RANGERS
SCRAPBOOK

Written By
Michael Leighton

sona BOOKS

First Published by Danann Media Publishing Limited 2021
© 2022 Danann Media Publishing Limited

WARNING: For private domestic use only, any unauthorised Copying, hiring, lending or public performance of this book set is illegal.

CAT NO: SONO537

Photography courtesy of The Press Association,
Getty Images;

Howard Boylan /Allsport	Bruno Ferrandez/AFP	Daily Record/Mirrorpix
Stuart Franklin /Allsport	John Chillingworth / Stringer	Paul Popper/Popperfoto
Mike Finn-Kelcey /Allsport	Imagno	Kevin John Berry/Fairfax Media
Jamie McDonald /Allsport	Jeff J Mitchell	Craig Williamson/SNS Group
Gary M Prior/Allsport	Transcendental Graphics	Andy Buchanan/AFP
Mark Thompson/Allsport	Mark Leech	Craig Foy/SNS Group
David Cannon	Ian MacNicol	SNS Group
David Cannon/Allsport	Werner OTTO/ullstein bild	Bill Murray/SNS Group
Stu Forster /Allsport	Mark Runnacles	Jeff Holmes/SNS Group
John Chillingworth	Staff/Mirrorpix	Paul Devlin - SNS Group
A. Hudson/Topical Press Agency	Bill Rowntree/Mirrorpix	Alan Harvey/SNS Group
Central Press	Randolph Caughie/Ian Elder/	
Christopher Lee	Mirrorpix	

ALAMY; PA Images

PA Images	BNA Photographic	Trinity Mirror/Mirrorpix
Maurice Savage	REUTERS	Allstar Picture Library Ltd

Book layout & design Darren Grice at **Ctrl-d**
Book design 2022 © Danann Media Publishing Limited
Copy Editor Tom O'Neill

All rights reserved. No Part of this title may be reproduced or transmitted in any material form (including photocopying or storing it in any medium by electronic means and whether or not transiently or incidentally to some other use of this publication) without the written permission of the copyright owner, except in accordance with the provisions of the Copyright, Designs and Patents Act 1988. Applications for the copyright owner's written permission should be addressed to the publisher.

Made in EU.
ISBN: 978-1-912918-97-3

the CONTENTS

INTRODUCTION 8
THE SCOTTISH FOOTBALL LEAGUE 12
A GARDENER'S FLOWERS OF SCOTLAND 16
A NEW ERA BEGINS 20
A DECADE OF STRUGGLE 22
AFTER THE GREAT WAR 26
PICKING UP THE PIECES 32
THE DOG-EARED YEARS 42
THAT MAN JOCK WALLACE 50
THE LEAGUE CUP BELONGS TO RANGERS 56
DOUBLES AND TREBLES GALORE! 62
SNAKES AND LADDERS 74
BACK TO THE FRONT 80
A KNIFE IN THE HEART 86
HERCULES McCOIST 88
GOODBYE CHAMPIONSHIP, HELLO NEW WORLD 92
FORWARD TO THE FUTURE 98
THE PLAYERS 102
THE MANAGERS 116
THE STATISTICS 122

INTRODUCTION

It is impossible to trace the exact origins of what evolved into the riveting sport known as football, the "beautiful game"; they are lost somewhere in the mists of memory that swirl around human activity as they may do on an autumn morning at Ibrox Stadium. So we must indulge in that wonderful pastime, speculation, spiced with some good, calculated guesses.

Whenever football is mentioned, Britain will be part of the conversation before long, so it is fitting that Britain has its part in the ancient folklore of the origins of the sport.

Local legends in both Chester and Kingston-on-Thames tell us that a game was played in those towns in which the amputated head of a defeated Danish prince, or a ruffian, which probably came to the same thing, was kicked around. That seems to be a good starting point; considering the curses from the terraces that wish a similar fate would befall the top goalscorers of opposing teams in the present-day game. In Derbyshire they would have us believe that Anglo-Saxon victory celebrations against the Romans brought on the desire to kick something else, as kicking the Romans had been such fun.

Long before that, written evidence supports the claim that the Romans and Greeks were instrumental in the game's birth. They played many ball games, as the Roman writer Cicero testified. One unfortunate man was killed whilst having a shave, wrote Cicero, when a ball came hurtling into the barber's shop where he was sitting. The Romans used ball games for more serious reasons, too. They were considered a good way to sharpen a soldier's reactions and spirit for battle.

The Chinese, inventive as they have always been, seem to have been ahead of the game as well. A form of football was played in the third and second centuries BC. during the Han dynasty, when people were already rushing around and kicking leather balls into a small net or through a hole in a piece of silk cloth stretched between two poles. It was probably played for the emperor's amusement. There is no record of what happened if he got bored, and relegation would not have been much fun back then. The game, as played by Chinese aristocrats, was known as t'su chu. But the Aztecs, Persians, Vikings and Japanese all had some form of ball game for entertainment. Luckily not against one another.

It was English peasants, however, who are said to be responsible for the increasing popularity of the game sometime around the 9th century AD. This old football game was a real free-for-all, and participants were allowed to bite, punch, stab and gouge as well as kick. Not much has changed in a thousand years after all. The ball had to be taken to a certain spot, and this game proved to be so popular that fields would be overflowing with eager sports fans. As you can imagine, it often got wildly out of hand. Archers would even sneak away from archery practice to watch.

Medieval Britain was undoubtedly the place where football began its unstoppable campaign. We still have an account of a match played in 1280; it took place in Northumberland, near Ashington. It's also the first report of a player being killed, when he ran onto the dagger worn by an opposing player. There is no report as to whether the dagger was in or out of the sheath at the time!

At what point the game reached Scotland is uncertain; there is no evidence that highlanders played it, so it may be that the game was brought in by players from France or England. In Scotland as in England, the medieval game involved not only kicking the ball, but also running whilst holding the ball, and scrummages. Team numbers might

INTRODUCTION

bulge alarmingly, numerically overwhelming the opposition. Not so very different to the game I saw last Saturday, then.

There is a present-day link to this early version of the game that is still played today; it can be found in Scotland. It's called Ba game. Depending on where the players were born they are either 'uppies' or 'downies', and the game flows around the streets of towns in the Scottish Borders and the Orkney Isles, in Duns, Scone, or Kirwall for example, at Christmas and New Year.

Incidents of violence became so frequent, in fact, that in 1365, King Edward III banned the game altogether. The ban was also an attempt to keep his archers at their practice (yes, they were still sneaking away from work) as their skills were sorely needed following the outbreak of the black plague that had decimated the population of the country.

King James I of Scotland, too, was very upset with the ruckus the ball game caused, and went even further, declaring in 1424 that, "Na man play at the Fute-ball". Perhaps his team kept losing. Whatever the cause, his 'Football Act' of 1424 outlawed football. Not to any great effect it would seem, if subsequent bans are anything to go by.

So by medieval times Scotland was already in the grip of football fever. Even royalty were eventually won over; in 1497, the king is known to have bought footballs, although there is no note of him playing the game himself.

James V is said to have gone to Jedburgh to take part in a game, though, but that story has never been properly confirmed.

Moving along another half century, dribbling and areas marked out to contain the field of play had come into existence, as the manuscript collection of the miracles of King Henry VI of England testifies:

". . . is called by some the foot-ball game. It is one in which young men, in country sport, propel a huge ball, not by throwing it into the air but by striking it and rolling it along the ground, and that not with their hands but with their feet . . ."

Scottish writers were now documenting this rumbustious sprawl, too; Gavin Douglas, in the years between 1501 and 1512 comments that;

"This broken shin that swells and will not be relieved, take it to him; he broke it at ball, and tell him it will be his reward. Take the whole of this bruised arm to him ..."

Sir Richard Maitland (Lord Lethington), whose father fell at the Battle of Flodden, was born in 1496. He was a Scottish lawyer, poet, and collector of Scottish verse. He also wrote satirical verses, and one of them, expressing his gratefulness that he will never have to play the game, runs:

"When young men come from the green,
Having been playing football,
Their shoulders broken,
I thank my God for failing eyesight,
I am so old."

In "The Bewties of the Fute-Ball", a sixteenth century Middle Scots writer uses humour to 'praise' the game;

"Brissit brawnis and brokin banis,

Stride, discord and waistie wanis.
Crukit in eild syne halt withal,
Thir are the bewties of the fute-ball."

("Torn muscles and broken bones,
Strife, discord and devastated homes,
Crooked in old age, limping, too,
Such are the beauties of football.")

King Henry VIII reputedly bought the first pair of football boots in 1526, and by 1546, the game was becoming so popular that the Scottish Company of Hammermen, the blacksmiths, had to order that "... neither servants nor apprentices 'play football', under penalty of a pound of wax". Well, either the lads used a lot of candles or they had very hairy wives; either way, you would not want to upset them!

Football had become much more organised by then. In 1581, English schools were providing reports of "parties" or "sides", "judges over the parties", and "training masters". But although the violence had lessened, it still raised its head. In 1595 a document stated: "Gunter's son and ye Gregorys fell together ... at football. Old Gunter drew his dagger and both broke their heads, and they died both within a fortnight after."

1606 saw similar clashes in Scotland; during a "fute-ball" match at Lochtoun, reports mention that some of the players "fell in contentioun and controversie, ilk anie with otheris, and schot and dilaschit pistolettis and hacquebuttis". You certainly needed a good marksman in your squad! A couple of 'lusty' full backs who didn't shirk from "contentioun and controversie" wouldn't have gone amiss either.

By the 1600s, football was an established and increasingly popular part of Scottish life, and references to it in the literature of the day became more frequent. In 1608, Shakespeare had King Lear say, "Nor tripped neither, you base football player". This was the first time "football" had been spelt in the modern manner.

" . . . lusty shepherds try their force at football, care of victory . . . They ply their feet, and still the restless ball,

FOOT-BALL.

toss'd to and fro, is urged by them all."

That was the Poet Edmund Waller (c.1624).
"The streete (in London) being full of footballs."
That was the famous diarist Samuel Pepys in 1665.

In Manchester in 1608, the local authorities complained that: "With the ffotebale . . . there hath beene greate disorder in our towne of Manchester we are told, and glasse windowes broken . . . by a companie of lewd and disordered persons using that unlawful exercise of playing with the ffotebale in ye streets of the said towne . . ."

Must have been visiting fans ...

In Scotland, Aberdeen schoolboys were now playing the game, too, apparently. It had not become any less violent and bore a great resemblance to modern rugby football. Those same Aberdeen youths incurred the disapproval of the Puritans, who accused them of profane behaviour on the Sabbath: " ... drinking, playing football ... and roving from parish to parish". The scowling was all to no avail, and even though the Puritans were less virulent in Scotland than in England, players in both countries blithely continued to enjoy the game. Here is evidence; in March 1648,

INTRODUCTION

Sir Patric Hume of Polwarth, Scotland, wrote to his wife. Their son, he said, had "... hurt himself so evill at football in Polwart upon Sunday that he was not able to sturre".

Not even an act passed by the Scottish Parliament in 1656 outlawing all boisterous games on the Lord's day produced the desired effect.

Football had come so far by 1660 that a book was written about it, the first objective study of the game in Britain. The author was Francis Willoughby, and he called his work, 'The Book of Sports'. It refers to goals and pitches, (goalkeeping had already been established by this time), to scoring and selecting teams and striking balls through goals. There is also a basic sketch of a football pitch and mention that a rule had been introduced so that players could not strike their opponent higher than the ball, otherwise they often "…. break one another's shins when two meet and strike together against the ball".

Even though football was often outlawed in many areas of the country with violators threatened with imprisonment, it remained popular even amongst aristocrats. "Lord Willoughby … with so many of their servants … play'd a match at foot-ball against such a number of countrymen, where my Lord of Sunderland being busy about the ball, got a bruise in the breast".

Football was really put on the map in 1681 when King Charles II of England attended a game between the Royal Household and the servants of George Monck, 1st Duke of Albemarle. Football was here to stay.

The Scottish novelist, poet and playwright, Sir Walter Scott, 1st Baronet, was born on the 15th of August 1771. He, too, felt the need to write about this violent sport. In the Lay, he writes: "In riot, revelry, and rout, Pursued the football, play". In "foot-ball", he continues, "The victory is contested with the utmost fury, and very serious accidents have sometimes taken place in the struggle".

In the 1800s, when the working man's day lasted twelve hours or more and six days a week, the only men who had enough leisure time to indulge in football were the wealthy. Certainly in Scotland in the early years of the 19th century, the Puritan bans on the game seemed to finally have an effect.

Boys at private schools, on the other hand, were encouraged to play to develop a competitive spirit and keep themselves fit, and so the rules developed that produced the game as we know it today.

Nonetheless, there were a variety of these rules regulating the matches, until in 1848, Mr. H. de Winton and Mr. J. C. Thring called a meeting at Cambridge University with twelve representatives from other schools; their eight-hour discussions produced the first set of modern rules, the Cambridge rules.

So in the truth, we have probably been throwing and kicking anything from monkey heads to coconuts and turnips since before we could walk upright. But there are at least 3,000 years of history behind the football match of today.

The millennia have passed and football, soccer, has become one of the most exciting mass entertainments of all time.

THE SCOTTISH

Clubs dedicated solely to the sport of football were formed regularly throughout the 19th century. The London Gymnastic Society was one of the first, created in the 1850s. The first club to be referred to as a club was the "Foot-Ball Club of Edinburgh" in Scotland in the period 1821 to 1824. Great Leicestershire Cricket and Football Club existed in 1840. The staff of Guy's Hospital in London formed Guys Hospital Football Club in 1843, which claims to be the oldest known football club, whilst Sheffield Football Club, founded in 1857, is the oldest club documented as not being affiliated to a school, university or other institution. The oldest club still playing association football is Cambridge University Association Football Club, which dates from 1856 or 1857.

In Scotland, the first clubs began to be formed in the late 1860s and in the 1870s. In 1867, for example, Queen's Park football club was founded in Glasgow. Queen's Park is now the oldest existing football club outside England, and it was the first to be formed in Scotland. Sheffield Wednesday was also formed in 1867.

Soon, club names that are recognisable to fans today were appearing; Dumbarton (1872), Rangers (1872), Heart of Midlothian (1874), Hibernian (1875), St. Mirren (1877), Aberdeen (1881), Motherwell (1886). Dundee came to the table relatively late, in 1893.

In England, it was finally decided that a set of rules was needed to which all clubs would adhere, and in 1862, thirteen London clubs met and hammered out regulations to govern the sport. This led to the formation of the Football Association in 1863 to oversee the administration of those regulations.

No history of football would be complete if the name of Ebenezer Cobb Morley was not mentioned. He was a central figure in bringing the Football Association into being. He was a player himself and a founding member of the Football Association. As captain of his team, the Barnes Club, he proposed a governing body for the sport, and so the meeting of the thirteen London clubs

ORIGINAL HANDWRITTEN RULES 1863

EBENEZER COBB MORLEY

FOOTBALL LEAGUE

came about. From 1863-1866 he was the FA's first secretary, and from 1867-1874 its second president. He drafted the "London Rules" at his home in Barnes in London.

Two momentous footballing events took place in 1873 in Scotland, the Scottish Cup was established, and the Scottish Football Association was formed – which means that it is now the second oldest national football association in the world – when the representatives of seven Scottish clubs gathered and agreed to form an association. With Kilmarnock sending a letter of intent to join, the clubs were; Queen's Park (Glasgow), on whose initiative the meeting took place, Clydesdale, Vale of Leven, Dumbreck, Third Lanark, Eastern and Granville.

Another event must be mentioned here: the first official, international game between England and Scotland took place on the 30th of November 1872 on the West of Scotland Cricket Ground in Partick, Scotland, in Glasgow's West End. 4,000 spectators watched a 0-0 draw, although the Scots had a goal disallowed. The very first game between the sides had taken place on the 5th of March 1870 at the Oval cricket ground in London. This was one of a series of four internationals. Scotland won their first international victory when they beat England 4-2 in Glasgow in 1874.

Most of the men playing in the teams at the time were amateurs, although betting had long been a feature of the sport. On the 18th of July 1885, it was finally decided that football could become a professional sport. But clubs were still setting their own fixture dates and the whole structure was chaotic. Now was the moment for another man to step into the limelight and make his mark on history; Mr. William McGregor, a director of Aston Villa Football Club. He had been raised in Scotland, in Perthshire, although for most of his life he had lived in Birmingham in England.

It was the 2nd of March 1888. McGregor wrote to the committees of several football clubs to propose a league competition that would guarantee a certain number of fixtures and bring some order into the confusion that still existed. In Anderson's Hotel in London on the 23rd of March 1888, on the eve of the FA Cup Final, a meeting was held to discuss the proposal. Manchester was once again in the headlines when on the 17th of April at the Royal Hotel, a final meeting created the Football League.

On the 8th of September 1888, twelve clubs, Accrington, Aston Villa, Blackburn Rovers, Bolton Wanderers, Burnley, Derby County, Everton, Notts County, Preston North End, Stoke, FC., West Bromwich Albion and Wolverhampton Wanderers, sent their players out onto the turf for the first games in the new Football League season.

Many Scottish players, the Scotch Professors as they were known, were moving south of the border, lured by the high salaries. So, soon after the formation of the English Football League, Peter Fairly, secretary of Renton Football Club, called a meeting of thirteen Scottish clubs. All the clubs except Queen's Park and Clyde attended. The year was 1890. On the 30th of April 1890, the Scottish Football League (SFL) was inaugurated. Rangers were present at the beginning of this historic era; together with ten other clubs they set out into that first season on the 23rd August 1890. Rangers' opponents were Abercorn, Cambuslang, Dumbarton, Heart of Midlothian, Celtic, Cowlairs, St. Mirren, Third Lanark, Vale of Leven, and Renton, who were expelled after five games for concealed professionalism... and then reinstated.

By 1893, the Scottish League had become professional anyway, and that same year a Second Division was added to accommodate the increasing number of clubs wishing to join. Many clubs came from the Scottish Alliance that had been set up in 1891.

In 1892, the English League also expanded with the addition of a new Second Division. Newcastle United joined the world of league football, as did Liverpool.

During 1898, the number of clubs in each English league increased to eighteen, and automatic promotion and relegation for two clubs was introduced the same year.

The Scottish Third Division was added in 1923, but it lasted only three years before collapsing with financial difficulties. From then on until after the Second World War, in 1946, there were only two Scottish leagues.

An English Third Division was only added after WWI, in 1921. By then, another host of well-known names, including Tottenham Hotspur and Fulham, had been added to the divisions, which by 1905 had been boosted in numbers to twenty clubs in each. There were two English third divisions, in fact; the Third Division North and the Third Division South.

With the coming of WWII, the league was suspended for seven seasons after the government banned all places of entertainment.

In post-war Scotland, there followed ten years in which the divisions were constantly renamed. The first, second and third divisions became A, B and C divisions. C division was split in 1949 to accommodate two sections; the North-West and the South-East. In 1955, there were only two divisions again, A and B, with 18 clubs in each. One year later, in 1956, divisions one and two had returned.

Over the border in England in 1950 there were twenty-four clubs in each of the two third divisions, so there were now ninety-two league clubs. The Third Division clubs were amalgamated into a single division, abolishing regionalisation, and the Fourth Division was added in 1958. Four clubs could be promoted and relegated in the lower two divisions. In divisions one and two, until 1974, two clubs made the climb, or fell; the number was increased to three that same year.

In Scotland, Division Two boasted twenty clubs in 1966 until Third Lanark left in 1967. From then until 1975 the division contained nineteen clubs. Division One operated with eighteen clubs.

In 1975 there was a major restructuring of the Scottish

divisions. There were now three; Premier, First, and Second, made up of thirty-eight clubs.

A period of calm had descended on the English league system with only minor changes occurring, such as altering the points system, three instead of two for a win, a measure introduced in 1981, and goal differences being taken into account. There was one enormous change ahead, however.

On May the 27th 1992, the Premier League was formed. All First Division clubs resigned together from the Football League, which now operated with three divisions. The old system of interaction between the leagues, however, did not change, but 104 years of tradition were over. The elite clubs were now, literally, in a league of their own. Money had tempted the top clubs, and lucrative television rights deals beckoned them. Those deals will soon exceed ten billion pounds.

After a period of relative calm in Scotland that lasted for two decades, the divisions were split into four with ten clubs in each; three points would be awarded for a win.

The calm didn't last long, though, for in 1998 the Scottish Premier League was formed above the First, Second and Third Divisions. There were just ten clubs in the Scottish Premier League, which expanded to twelve in the year 2000. Forty-two clubs were now competing in the Scottish League.

And there was more adjustment to come. From 2005, there were promotion and relegation play-offs between the second, third and fourth-placed clubs in a lower division, and the club placed second from bottom in the higher division. None of the clubs that found themselves at the very foot of the Third Division, were relegated.

One more change was agreed upon. In 2013 the Scottish Football Association and the Scottish Premier League voted to merge and form the Scottish Professional Football League. The divisions are now known as; the Scottish Premiership, Scottish Championship, Scottish League One, Scottish League Two. All forty-two member clubs of the SPFL are owners of the SPFL corporation, having voting rights on a variety of issues concerning contract and rule changes.

In both Scotland, and especially England, the wealth, of course, makes it almost impossible for a promoted club to compete with the big boys in the first season after promotion. But the rewards for the successful are enormous. Clubs like Rangers are amongst the richest in the world and able to buy in players who make the terraces on a Saturday afternoon one of the most thrilling places to be.

SCOTTISH FA CUP MATCH, IBROX, GLASGOW, SCOTLAND, 6TH MARCH 1971

A GARDENER'S FLOWERS

Without a doubt, Rangers FC owes its creation to the passionate spirit that has subsequently brought the team to the very top echelons of the football world. The 1800s was an era of terrible hardship with poverty rife and education prospects limited for many of the people of Glasgow – 4,750 children under the age of five died in Glasgow in 1888.

But the inauspicious beginnings for the later fame and glory of Rangers FC were rooted in this difficult time, for it was in the mid-1880s that a gardener, John McNeil, and his wife Jane Loudon Bain gave life to two brothers, Peter, born in 1854 (died the 30th of March 1901) and brother Moses, born on the 29th of October 1855 (died on the 9th of April 1938), both boys first seeing the light of day in Rhu on the east shore of Gare Loch (Gareloch) in Argyll and Bute, Scotland. (Well, to be honest, Peter fist saw the light of day through the windows of Belmont House in Rhu, Dumbartonshire, where his father was the gardener.) Had the family stayed in Rhu there probably would not have been a Rangers FC. in Glasgow. But fortunately they didn't, because in about 1870, dad and mum McNeil decided to up sticks and take off for Anderston, the former centre of 18th-century handloom weavers on the north bank of the River Clyde, south and west of the city centre. There, they came to rest at no. 17 Cleveland St. Some time around one year later, Peter became an apprentice clerk in the town. (There were, by they way, ten children born to John and Jane in all, two of whom died at a very young age.) In an age of rapid industrialisation in Glasgow, many families left the Scottish countryside and smaller towns to seek their fortune in Glasgow, the Second City of the British Empire. It was a city heading for a population of one million souls that was grimly and gloomily marked by the shipbuilding, steel and engineering industries that were feeding and fed by British imperial ambition.

Thus could it come about that in 1872, Peter, then the eldest of the group at seventeen years of age, and

WILLIAM MCBEATH

PETER CAMPBELL

RANGERS FC CIRCA 1877

younger brother Moses, then a teenager of sixteen, could be walking in Kelvingrove Park (known in those days as West End Park) in the West End of Glasgow with their mates Peter Campbell, who was fifteen and another lad from Rhu, (Peter died in 1883 when he drowned after his ship, the Saint Columba, sailing from south Wales to Bombay with a cargo of coal, sank during a storm in the Bay of Biscay), and William McBeath, also fifteen from Callander in Perthshire. William's mother had moved to Glasgow when her son was eight not long after his father had died. William was out working by the age of fourteen and known to have been a salesman. He lived in, yes, of course, Cleveland St.

Touching on the subject that will inevitably raise its head, there's nothing to suggest that religious affiliation had anything to do with the founding members' thought process when they formed their team; their united love

OF SCOTLAND

of football was their sole driving motivation, although it must be assumed that the lads were brought up as Protestants.

As they sauntered along chatting about football, the idea crystallised; perhaps they could form their own team. Enthusiastically they searched for a name for the fledgling team and Moses came up with Rangers. It was a name that had appealed to him ever since he'd seen it mentioned in a manual about English rugby. Easy to see that Moses, who was to become the most prominent of the four friends in the history of Rangers FC, had been a keen sportsman from an early age.

Victorian Britain was falling for association football in a big way. Saturday afternoon was free time from the sweat-drenched graft in the heavy industry sites, and football was an ideal way to let off steam and have a few hours of entertainment and excitement. The game itself was still an amateur sport and far from gaining any kind of proper organisation. It was against this societal backdrop that Rangers was created sometime in March 1872. No sooner created than the four friends had put together a team; Rangers was born.

In May 1872, they stepped out to do battle with Callander FC at Flesher's Haugh, part of Glasgow Green and a famous landmark, as this was where Bonnie Prince Charlie's army set up camp from the 25th of December 1745 until the 3rd of January 1746. Callander FC went in the opposite direction to Rangers and vanished from the history books. Rangers, on the other hand, has just celebrated 150 years of football, the first major club in Europe to be in existence for that length of time. An extraordinary achievement in itself.

That first Rangers team had to fill out the squad with players borrowed from other teams, and the two McNeil's brother, Harry, was drafted into the side as well. Harry was also one of the only men, along with Willie McKinnon (like Harry a Queen's Park player) and Eastern players John Hunter and Willie Miller not to play in their workday clothes. Peter Campbell and Moses McNeill were in the forward line up, with Peter McNeill taking up a position in midfield. Also in the team was another founder member, David Hill, who was out on the wing.

William was part of the defence and apparently so energetic during the game that he was said to have spent the next week in bed recovering. Who's to say? But that passion has never died in the Rangers' teams to this day. The four lad's heroic efforts didn't help to produce a win, however, and the historic game ended in a 0-0 draw. Perhaps Willy and the lads had overdone it, for Rangers only took part in one more game that year. But when they left the pitch after the game against Clyde (not the forerunner of the present-day Clyde club), they had won 11-0.

The year following formation of the club, 1873, the year that also saw the club's first annual meeting, the lads had decided on club colours and would now play in blue. From then on, a solid blue shirt was a constant fixture, except for the years between 1879 and 1883 when a collective brain meltdown saw the team dazzle spectators in blue and white hooped shirts and socks. Likewise, white shorts and black and red-topped socks have been predominant throughout the club's history.

Another year on and the Rangers' story truly began to take shape as the club entered its first year of competitive football, the first games in the Scottish Cup. They beat Oxford 2-0, one scored by Moses NcNeil, but fell to Dumbarton in the second leg of the second round, losing 1-0. The historic team was as follows: John Yuil, Tom Vallance, Peter McNeil, William McNeil, Willie McBeath, Moses McNeil, Peter Campbell, George Phillips, James Watson, David Gibb, John Campbell.

Rangers, who had found their own ground in 1875, Burnbank, near Kelvin Bridge, now boasted an international in their ranks; Moses had played for the Scottish national team against Wales. The 'Light Blues' also managed to get to two Scottish Cup finals over the remainder of that decade, the first in 1877 when Rangers were beginning to see spectator interest in the club increase. Two 1-1 draws, saw Rangers and Vale of Leven, one of Scotland's best, clash a third time, Rangers going down 3-2. But having tasted the big time, they were not about to let it go.

The second final came in the 1978-79 season, but a disallowed goal against old enemies Leven so angered the team that they refused to attend the replay.

By then, Rangers had moved again, to Kinning Park, and revenge came in that same season, one month later, when Leven were defeated 2-1 in the Glasgow Merchant's Charity Cup at Hampden; another historic first.

HARRY MCNEIL

A NEW ERA

Rangers entered the 1880s as a successful team with a bright future despite the departure of some of the big names in the team, but they didn't manage to get back into another Scottish Cup final. They did enter the English FA Cup in 1885-86, not an unusual move for a Scottish club. Their best result was a 5-1 victory against Old Westminsters, but there was to be no glory in the final there, either. And from 1883, the appointment of a controversial John Wallace MacKay, who took over as secretary and whose influence almost downed the club until he was forced out in 1866, didn't help.

Moses McNeil retired in 1882, concentrating on his work as a commercial traveller. That Glasgow Merchant's Charity Cup proved to be his only honour, but his place in Rangers' history was assured.

The next historic event was just around the corner; the 20th of August 1887 saw the powerful English side Preston North End, the 'Invincibles', travel to Rangers' new ground at Ibrox Park, which was an icon in the making. And duly inaugurated with a cold shower; an 8-1 defeat was not the start to a new shining future for Rangers that everyone had hoped for.

The date, the 28th May 1888. The occasion; the first game against Celtic, formed the previous year. It was a friendly and Rangers took a bit of hiding, 5-2 from a team that for the most part consisted of Hibernian players.

That defeat was to herald a period of great instability for the club as the 1888-89 season brought 19 defeats in 39 matches for the Light Blues. An even greater defeat to Celtic in the Glasgow Cup, 6-1 left the club reeling on the field and facing bankruptcy off the field.

Managing to stay afloat nonetheless, Rangers became one of the founding members of the new Scottish League, created in the 1890-91 season. Under the guidance of match secretary William Walton, Rangers were lined up beside the other clubs signing up for the new league competition; Celtic, Heart of Midlothian, Saint Mirren, Third Lanark, Renton, Dumbarton, Cowlairs, Vale of Leven, Abercorn and Cambuslang.

Rangers got off to an inspiring start in an inspiring season for Scottish football. They thrashed Hearts in their first league game on the 16th of August 1890, 5-2 at home. The only blemish that season were the defeats to Celtic and Dumbarton, although Rangers had won 13 games of the 18 they had played. After a play-off, Rangers and Dumbarton ended the season with 29 points each. Striker John McPherson was the top goalscorer, bagging 15. He would go on to net 98 goals for Rangers in his 175 appearances for the Gers.

From now on, Rangers were a force to be reckoned with in a game that was rapidly entering the professional era. Runners-up in the league in the 1892-93 (a second league tier was added that season), 1895-96 and 1896-97 seasons.

But they had won the Scottish Cup on the 17th of February 1894 with a famous victory over arch rivals Celtic, 3-1, and the next cup victory, in the 1896-1897 season, was the start of a period of enormous success for Rangers. Having smacked Green Rock Morton out of the park in the semi-final on the 13th of March 1896, 7-2, they took another cup victory on the 20th of March when they had the enormous satisfaction of belting five past Dumbarton in a 5-1 victory. McPherson again added two goals to Rangers' tally.

The following season, whilst climbing to 2nd in the league with matches that included a 9-0 hammering of St. Mirren, they again took the Scottish Cup putting two past Kilmarnock in front of the 14,000 crowd. The next Scottish Cup win would not come until the 1902-03 season, but by then fans had been treated to the team taking the league honours in four successive and thrilling league seasons.

RANGERS FC, 1896-97

The run started in the extraordinary 1889-1900 season as Rangers finished the 19th century to take their first Scottish League Division One title as sole champions. Once again, they produced a sheaf of top results; 6-2 and 5-0 against Partick Thistle, 8-0 against Clyde, 9-0 against Dundee, 10-0 against Hibernian. Rangers won every league match that season and defeated Celtic twice, 4-0 and 4-1, at that time an unequalled achievement.

It was striker Robert Hamilton whose name popped up again and again on the hit list, and he became top goalscorer that season with 25 to his credit. Hamilton would take the top goalscorer credit for an amazing nine successive seasons, his best tally being 26 goals, a feat unmatched until the 1914-15 season. Hamilton also struck three times during the Scottish Cup run, although Rangers succumbed in the final to Celtic 0-2.

Rangers Football Club Ltd. was born on the 27th May 1899, with a board of directors and William Wilton taking on the manager and secretary roles. So with players earning a majestic £2 per week, Rangers set off into the new century full of confidence.

Celtic, who else, were spoilers again in an otherwise undefeated season ending in 1900, carrying off a 3-3 draw, a 3-2 win and taking another win from the Scottish Cup semi-final replay 0-4. Rangers' revenge, though, was to take their second successive league title.

And then a third in 1901 when they dropped an unprecedented two games! But they were still winning matches in spectacular style; 4-0 (Third Lanark), 5-1 (Kilmarnock) and 6-0 (Hibernian).

A DECADE

Success was becoming a habit for Rangers, but the year brought sad news as well. On March the 30th of 1901, Peter McNeil, one of the founding fathers of the club, died aged 47 at the Hawkhead Asylum near Paisley. Having ended his football career in 1877, his mental and physical well-being had suffered severely from the financial difficulties he went through. It was a sad end for a man who had been instrumental in those important early years for Rangers. He was buried in Creighton Cemetery in the south-west of Glasgow.

Otherwise, Rangers entered the 1901-1902 season with high hopes for more success and fans were not disappointed. Despite the fact that it was their least successful season in terms of matches won since the 1894-95 season they still took the title. But five losses and two draws and the least number of points, 28, that they would ever gain (excluding the 1939 to 1940 season when the world turned to insanity and away from football) turned out to be unwelcome heralds of a greater malaise to come.

From 1902 until 1910, Rangers struggled to keep within sight of the league leaders, only hitting second place once in 1904-1905. Neither were there any Scottish Cup successes to offset the failures. Greatest sensation of those years was the Scottish Cup Final in 1909, when Rangers and Celtic lined up against one another only to produce a 2-2 draw in the final and a 1-1 draw in the replay. It was the suspicion that these two mighty clubs might have actually rigged the matches so that they could enjoy another money-spinning replay that caused fans to invade the pitch and riot for the next three hours, during which time the goalposts were dragged down, sections of the pitch were ripped up and wooden pay-boxes were set on fire. Six people were seriously injured and 130 suffered minor injuries. The Old Firms, as the clubs had been

RANGERS FC 1902

RANGERS FC 1905-06

OF STRUGGLE

known since the beginning of the century, were fined £150 each. But their domination of Scottish football was already clear for all to see and continues up to the present day. Rangers would never again suffer such a drought of awards as they now had put behind them.

As the club and the world hurtled unwittingly towards the First World War, Rangers suddenly found their form again when the 1910–1911 season got underway. Despite five defeats, they eventually sailed up to take the league title with 52 points and repeated the trick over the next two seasons bringing home 51 points and 53 points respectively. That season of 1912-1913 was slightly strange; Celtic had been hot on the lads' heels and defeated them twice in the league and yet finished three points behind them at the end of the season. It was also the season of the short-lived Inter City Midweek Football League, which consisted of six top SFL clubs but which was abandoned in November 1912 due to poor attendances. But not before Rangers had flattened Celtic 4-0.

Round 3 in the Scottish Cup, losing 1-3 to Falkirk was not one to write home about, however.

A DECADE OF STRUGGLE

RANGERS FC CIRCA 1912

Rangers could not pull the iron out of the fire in that final season before war engulfed everyone. They finished second in the league, Willie Reid becoming top goalscorer again, a feat he accomplished for six successive seasons before the war interrupted his life, as it did for so many others, in 1916. Reid then joined the Royal Field Artillery 52nd Lowland Division as a gunner, but survived and returned for the 1919-1920 season. Outside left Jimmy Paterson was a medical doctor and joined the Royal Medical Corps Attached 1/14th (County of London) Battalion (London Scottish) and was awarded The Military Cross, "For conspicuous gallantry and devotion to duty".

Some, like former player Alexander Barrie, would not return home. Barrie joined the Highland Light Infantry 17th (Service) Battalion (3rd Glasgow) Second Battalion and was killed in action in Western Europe on the 1st of October 1918.

Amongst those heroes of the football pitch who joined up to heroically serve their country were the following players, who were either playing for the club at the time or had played for the club in the past:

Sandy Archibald, Andy Cunningham, Scott Duncan, John Fleming, Jimmy Gordon, Fred Gray, John McCulloch, Tommy Muirhead, Jimmy Patterson, William Reid, Alexander Barrie, Alex Bennett, Jackie Boville, John Clark, Bob Dalrymple, Jimmy Galt, Tom Gilchrist, Billy Henry, Willie Kivlichan, Jimmy Lister, George Livingston, David Murray († 1915. Princess Louise's Argyll & Sutherland Highlanders), Bobby Parker, John Rankin, Jimmy Sharp, Tom Sinclair, Finley Speedie, Jamie Speirs († 1917. Queen's Own Cameron Highlanders), Jimmy Stewart, Sandy Tate, and David Taylor.

AFTER THE GREAT

The Scottish Cup was abandoned when war broke out, but the clubs played on in the league despite losing players to the front lines of the Western Front. They were unsuccessful years for Rangers in their attempts to regain the top of the division, until the final year of the war when they once again claimed the top spot in 1917–1918, squeaking home just one point ahead of Celtic.

For the lads from Rangers, the torments of war behind them, there now began an extraordinary round of league successes that would carry them all the way through the interwar years with seemingly unstoppable momentum until 1939 when war once again unleashed its horrors upon Scotland and the rest of Europe.

From the 1919-20 season until the abandonment of the 1939-1940 games, Rangers won the Scottish League Division One title 15 times. They were third once, second three times, and had a club-wide mental seizure in 1926 when they came 6th. Not sure how else to explain that one! The big hitters who became top goalscorers were Geordie Henderson, four times, Jimmy Fleming four times (plus becoming top goalscorer along with Andy Cunningham during that season of 1925-1926) and Jimmy Smith, who took the honours six times.

Their runaway best season as far as points were concerned was the 1928-1929 season when they came home top of the league with 67. They hammered 8 past St. Johnstone, 7 past Raith Rovers, won a whole swathe of matches scoring 4 and 5 goals at a time and downed Celtic twice, winning 3-0 the second time in front of a 60,000 crowd. With 60 points, Rangers took the title ahead of Celtic on 55.

But the crowning glory of that season was without doubt the day of the Scottish Cup Final. Lining up against Celtic one final time that year, in front of a crowd of 118,000 people, the match became a shining beacon in the history

AFTER THE GREAT WAR

GLASGOW RANGERS WIN AGAINST THE SK RAPID 3:1, AUGUST 15TH 1934

WAR

Fortunately for Rangers, however, Wilton's successor proved to have the Midas touch. Another William took over managership of the club, although he was best known as Bill; Bill Struth. Bill became a legend and one of the most successful Scottish or British football managers of all time. And what an incredible haul of trophies he brought to Ibrox Park; 18 Scottish League Championships, a record; 10 Scottish Cup victories, and 2 Scottish League Cup victories.

Mighty Bill Struth not only guided Rangers to 14 of the 15 inter-war Scottish league victories, there were also six Scottish Cup victories during those years as well, five of those helping to create Ranger's double victories. What absolutely brilliant achievements.

In 1938, another of the four men who had founded the club and so acquired the nickname the Gallant Pioneers, Moses McNeil, passed away in Dumbarton at the age of 82. McNeil had also won 2 caps playing for Scotland and had become a commercial traveller once he

of Rangers football club. Davie Meiklejohn, the Gers captain, found himself about to take a penalty and thus facing the possibility of breaking the awful run of Scottish Cup bad luck. Knowing that if he scored it was likely that the spell would be broken, he struck the ball at one minute past 2 o'clock... and Rangers were on their way to a roaring win. Bob McPhail and Sandy Archibald, twice, took their cue to emphatically finish off Celtic with a 4-0 hiding. What a glorious day to be a Rangers fan. McPhail would eventually become one of the most efficient forwards ever at Ibrox, scoring 261 by the time he stopped playing in 1940, twelve years later.

It was off the pitch that the club experienced emotional sadness during those exciting years. Ranger's first manager, William Wilton, the man who had seen the colours of Rangers shine in 881 matches, tragically died in a boating accident on the 2nd of May 1920.

AFTER THE GREAT WAR

had hung up his boots. The cause of death was heart disease. He was buried at Rosneath.

William McBeath had been forgotten by the football world. Since leaving Rangers, the final seven years of his life had taken place in a poorhouse in Lincoln. It seems that Alzheimer's was responsible, not a disease understood at the time. His last day on earth was Sunday the 15th of July 1917. Finally released from his penury, he found his final resting place in an unmarked grave in a cemetery in Lincoln.

With another war around the corner, Ranger's founding fathers, the original four friends, had left the club forever. It truly was the end of an era.

Once again, with the league suspended, Rangers players left the blue shirts behind them to don haversacks and march off with the armies of Britain. Those remaining played in unofficial non-competitive football matches, most of which were won by Rangers.

RANGERS TEAM CAPTAIN, J SIMPSON, LEADS HIS TEAM OUT FOR A MATCH AGAINST ARSENAL AT HIGHBURY DURING THE SCOTTISH TEAM'S TOUR OF THE SOUTH, 24TH SEPTEMBER 1936

WORLD WAR TWO

SOCCER MAY SHUT DOWN UNTIL PEACE

RANGERS PLAYERS SERVING IN THE BRITISH ARMY:

- Willie Thornton (Scottish Horse Regiment – awarded the Military Medal for "acts of gallantry and devotion to duty under fire". (In Sicily on the 18th of November 1943.)
- Donald McLatchie (Gunner – Royal Artillery)
- Thomas Souter (Captain – Royal Scots Fusiliers)
- Sammy Cox (Gordon Highlanders)
- David Gray (served in the Middle East)
- Archie Macauley (Army Physical Training Corps)
- Willie Paton
- David Marshall
- David Kinnear
- 'Torry' Gillick
- Dr. Adam Little
- Eddie Rutherford
- Jimmy Galloway
- Alex McKillop
- Tom McKillop
- Joe Johnston
- Willie Knox
- R. Cowan
- P. Grant
- A. Beattie
- GDF Mackay.

RANGERS PLAYERS SERVING IN THE RAF

Chris McNee - Flight Lieutenant

Ian McPherson (awarded the Distinguished Flying Cross in June 1944, by which time he had flown 57 sorties over enemy territory. McPherson was promoted to Flying Officer and was awarded a Bar to add to his DFC in January 1945 after 102 sorties. The final part of his recommendation read: "... he has consistently displayed exemplary courage and tenacity of purpose, which, together with outstanding skill and fine leadership, are worthy of high praise".

Eddie Rutherford
Jimmy Simpson
Alex Stevenson

RANGERS PLAYERS SERVING IN THE ROYAL NAVY:

Jimmy Parlane
Billy Williamson
Bobby Brown
(joined Rangers post-WW2)-(Petty Officer-Fleet Air Arm.)

JOCK SHAW LEADS OUT THE RANGERS TEAM, FOLLOWED BY DAWSON BEFORE THE CLYDE V RANGERS GLASGOW CUP SEMI-FINAL HELD AT SHAWFIELD PARK, 24TH SEPTEMBER 1945

PICKING UP THE

Post WW2, and with the introduction of the League Cup in 1946, Bill Struth and Willie Thornton settled back into their old roles and winning ways at Rangers, Thornton becoming top goalscorer for five of the next six seasons, sharing the honours with Jimmy Duncanson in the 1946-47 season.

This was the era when Rangers fans would speak in awe about the 'Iron Curtain', and they were not talking about the metaphorical one separating European states. This Iron Curtain consisted of Jerry Dawson, Scot Symon, Dougie Gray, George Young, Jock Shaw and Sammy Cox. They were the Rangers defenders and midfielders, more formidable than the Warsaw Pact to any opposing team.

Bill Struth oversaw his team's victory in the inaugural final of the League Cup, Rangers beating Aberdeen 4-0 and finishing on the top spot for three of the next four seasons in Division A. During this period, Rangers also won the Scottish Cup three times in a row starting in the 1947-48 season, and the League Cup for a second time in the 1948-49 season; that made eight trophies in four seasons.

Rivals Celtic presented little problem to the new confidence of the Rangers team in those years. In fact, Rangers trounced them 4-0 on more than one occasion and Celtic had to wait until the 23rd of September 1950 to squeeze a 2-3 victory from the boys in blue. It was Hibernian who presented more of a problem, and indeed, it was Hibernian who took the title for the 1947-48 season pipping Rangers to the post by two points with a tally of 48. Having beaten Hibernian earlier in the season 2-1, Rangers could reasonably have expected to claim the title again that year. But when they

conceded a goal away from home and then won only four of the remaining 10 games in the season, that defeat, together with four others, was enough to see them yield the top spot to Hibernian.

Rangers returned with a vengeance the following season to sweep the board and claim the 1948-49 Treble (Scottish League, Scottish Cup and the League Cup). And Willy Thornton scored hat-tricks in both the league and the Scottish Cup

CELTIC GOALKEEPER MILLER FAILS TO KEEP THE BALL OUT OF THE NET AFTER A PENALTY KICK BY WILLIAM WADDELL OF RANGERS AT IBROX STADIUM, GLASGOW, 15TH OCTOBER 1949

PIECES

RANGERS F.C. 1958-59
Left to right (Back row) McILROY, BRAND, ORR, CURRIE, NIVEN, LITTLE, MARTIN, MOLES, AUSTIN, WILSON, McCORQUODALE; (Middle row) Mr. Scot Symon (Manager), MILLAR, SMITH, SIMPSON, VALENTINE, BAIRD, PATERSON, TELFER, DAVIES, HOGG, NEIL, MURRAY, CRAVEN (Asst. trainer); (Front row) DUNCAN, SCOTT, QUEEN, SHEARER, McEWAN, McCOLL, STEVENSON, CALDOW, MATTHEWS, HUBBARD, PROVAN.

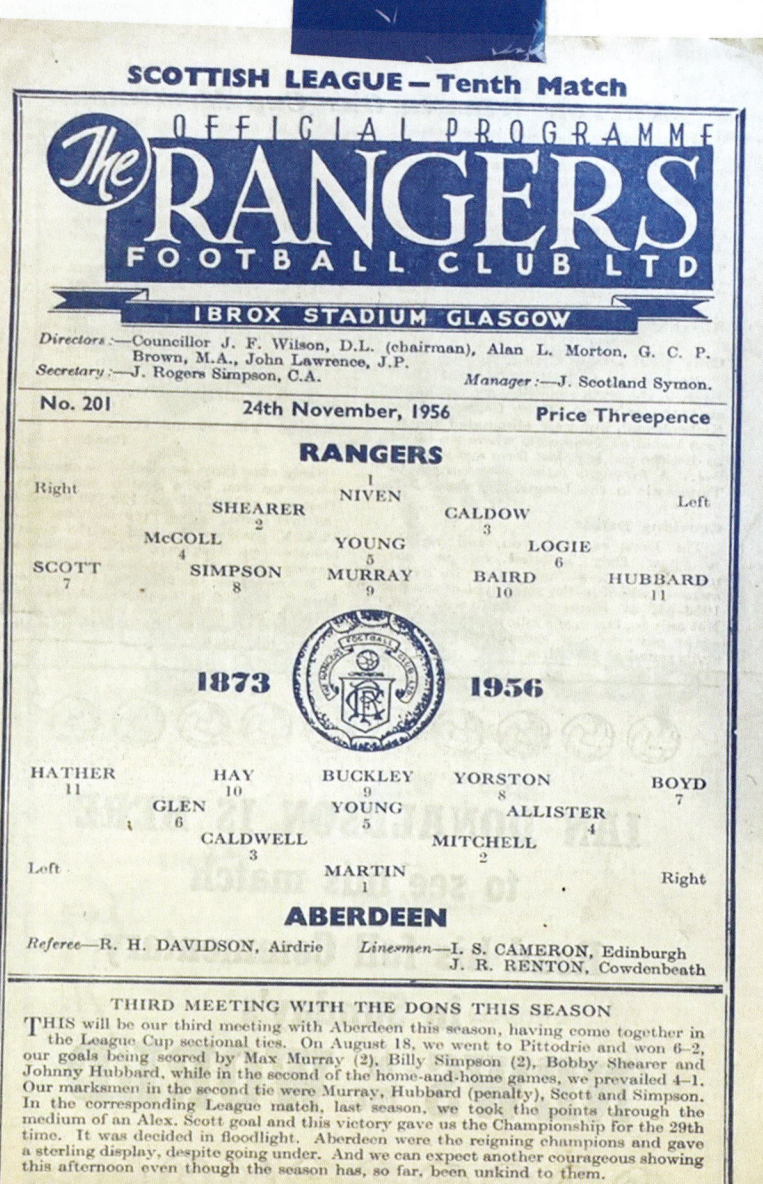

competitions to help the club on its way to glory. The warriors of that special year deserve their mention: goalkeeper Bobby Brown; defenders Sammy Cox, John Lindsey, Ian McColl and Corky Young; midfielders Adam Little, Willie Woodburn; forwards Jimmy Caskie, Torri Gillick, Willie Thornton and Willie Waddle. And not forgetting, of course, the man at the helm, William Struth.

With the onset of the 1950-51 season, when Hibernian again took the league title 10 points ahead of Rangers, who claimed just 38, the club slightly lost its way and brought in a series of disappointing results for the following nine seasons. Disappointing for a club of the calibre of Rangers, that is, because it was not a period entirely bereft of hardware. There were four league titles, one League Cup and one Scottish Cup to boast about. The legendary Willie Thornton was able to see the club bring home another league and Scottish Cup double in the 1952-53 season before calling it a day in 1954, by which time he had yielded the top goalscorer position to Derek Grierson and then Willie Paton.

PICKING UP THE PIECES

EVANS OF CELTIC (LEFT) AND COX OF GLASGOW RANGERS COMPETE FOR THE BALL DURING A DERBY MATCH AT IBROX STADIUM, GLASGOW, 1949

1950: GLASGOW RANGERS FOOTBALLERS, JOCK SHAW (LEFT) AND WILLIAM WADDELL

GLASGOW RANGERS V HIBERNIAN, 1956

But the main focus of attention was, of course, on the man who was in charge, Bill Struth. With results failing to live up to expectations, the question on everyone's lips was, was the manager still up to the job? Fans and press alike began to voice their concerns and disapproval. But no one could find the courage to persuade him to go.

Finally, when Rangers ended fourth in the 1953-54 season, he saw that the writing was on the wall and brought to an end an unprecedented era of successful Rangers' seasons by resigning and handing over the hot seat to James Symon, who had played at wing-half for Rangers between the years of 1938 and 1947. Symon would lead Rangers through to 1967, and along the way gain his own considerable reputation; six League Championships, five Scottish Cups, and four League Cups besides guiding the club into European football for the first time and into two Cup Winners' Cup finals. He would also preside over another domestic treble in the 1963-64 season – but more about that in good time.

These were the years of magnificent players such as right back Eric Caldow, who captained both Rangers and Scotland, right half Harold Davis, Johnny Hubbard, one of a handful of players to gain a hat-trick against Celtic (1st of January 1955) and who acquired the nickname of the "Penalty King" with his outstanding 65-goal record from 68 penalty attempts of which 22 were consecutive, and the magnificent George Young, a 16-year faithful at Rangers and the first player to be capped over 50 times for the Scotland squad.

Nonetheless, it would take Symons five seasons to get Rangers back to their double-winning ways.

But the trophies weren't that scarce, either. This was Rangers, after all. The Gers hit the top spot in the league in the 1955-56 season banishing both Hibernian and Celtic to the depths and repeating the trick the following season, trouncing each opponent

twice in the league, Hibernian getting walloped 5-3 and 3-2 in thrilling encounters. That season was also the first in which the club entered the European Cup competition, then in its second year, though getting only as far as the second round before being knocked out by Nice. Success in that competition would elude Rangers until the 1970s. There was another league title in 1958-59, and after a drought of six seasons with no League Cup or Scottish Cup success,

a Scottish Cup win finally arrived in 1960, the competition's 75th year.

Rangers faced Kilmarnock, a team they had made mincemeat out of in the league with a 5-1 thrashing, so confidence was on Rangers' side as they set out to finally crack the curse. With Jimmy Millar and Ralph Brand forming a formidable partnership on the field, it was Millar who was there to bring in the results for Rangers with two goals at full time (having also struck two in the 4-1 crushing of Celtic in the replay of the semi-final).

Well, it has to be mentioned because it was a milestone, though of the wrong sort. Yes, it's about that European Cup final against German club

GUARDIANS OF IBROX

EUROPEAN CUP

TOTTENHAM HOTSPUR

v.

GLASGOW RANGERS

WHITE HART LANE
WEDNESDAY, 31st OCT. 1962
KICK OFF 7.45 p.m.

SOUVENIR PROGRAMME

Eintracht Frankfurt, so let's make this short. Rangers had fought their way through to the semi-final of the European Cup. Only to suffer a communal meltdown. When captain Caldow equalised two minutes after the Germans had scored, all still seemed to be well. But then the floodgates opened and Rangers conceded another five goals to leave the field 6-1 in arrears. They left themselves a herculean task for the replay second leg, but up until the 20th minute they were level pegging with Frankfurt, 1-1. And then history repeated itself, almost, and at full time the Germans had bagged another 6, against 3 for Rangers. Alex Scott thought that tactical shortcomings had been the undoing of his team, "but we only knew how to play one way and that was to go forward". Alright, enough pain.

That Scottish Cup win seemed to lend wings to the Rangers team, and over the next four seasons they set off into an unprecedented

PICKING UP THE PIECES

SPARTA VS. GLASGOW RANGERS FOR THE EUROPA CUP I (2-3). ELVES ENTER THE FIELD PRECEDED BY A BAGPIPE PLAYER, 9 MARCH 1960

blazing series of three doubles and a treble. There were three Scottish Cups, three League Cups and two Division One titles to add to the already impressive history book entries. The Gers produced some of the most scintillating football ever against a host of keen opposition besides Celtic; Dundee, Hibs, Aberdeen, Kilmarnock or Motherwell. Possibly the Rangers teams of the early 1960s were unmatched throughout Scotland. But then the team did boast the likes of left-half 'Slim' Jim Baxter, regarded as one of the best players, not only at Rangers, but in the entire country of Scotland.

Of the myriad of outstanding performances, too numerous to mention, one game can be singled out to highlight Rangers' magnificent achievements of that time. It was the season of the triple, 1963-64, the season when Jim Forrest was top goalscorer for the first time with 39. It was the season of the 5-0 hammering of Morton in the League Cup final, the season of 4 league games when Rangers scored five goals in each and six games when they had put away four on each occasion; when Rangers sailed to the top of the league with 55 points and Celtic were nowhere in sight, the season when Rangers proved their quality in another Scottish Cup final. Against Dundee.

RANGERS SCRAPBOOK

TOTTENHAM HOTSPUR V GLASGOW RANGERS EUROPEAN CUP 1962

120,000 spectators watched the game and Rangers were relentless in attack, but they were given plenty of frights by a dogged Dundee eleven and were thwarted time and time again by Dundee goalie Bert Slater, who seemed to possess supernatural powers as he hurled himself around the goalmouth and helped the scoreline to stay 0-0 at half time.

It took a cracking header by Millar to break the stalemate only for Dundee to also put one away. Rangers refused to be downhearted but had to fight all the way to the 90th minute before Millar released the tension, again with his head. And when Ralph Brand (twice top goalscorer for the club with 40 goals each season) soared in to twist and put the result beyond doubt from a position almost parallel to the goal line, it was no more than a storming Rangers deserved in a game that had proven the metal and staying

OFFICIAL PROGRAMME
RANGERS v. MORTON
SCOTTISH LEAGUE CUP FINAL
PRICE 6D.
Kick-off 3 p.m.
SATURDAY, 26th OCTOBER 1963
HAMPDEN PARK · GLASGOW

PICKING UP THE PIECES

power that had made them triple champions. Let's not forget, either, those other giants of that team, especially two midfielders; 'Wee' Willie Henderson, 5' 4" in height, who joined forces with Jim Baxter to produce effervescent football that could make your spine tingle. Both men were unique individuals who ploughed their own furrow and became two more idols of the Rangers' 60s era.

THE DOG-EARED

In the mid-sixties, Rangers hit an uncharacteristic soft spot, and for the next decade not a single league title came their way. Gone the days of doubles and triples. Indeed, for a large chunk of the remainder of the 60s, gone were trophies of any kind. The 1964-65 season started off with two defeats in the first four games, one of them to Celtic 3-1, and they had to wait until the fifth match for the first victory, which, happily, was one of those Rangers' goal feasts with a whopping 9-2 dismantling of Airdrieonians. But there were several more defeats waiting for later in the season and the lads finished on a dismal 5th league place, although a mere 6 points behind champions Kilmarnock who had 50. Neither was there any joy in the Scottish Cup or the European Cup, so there was only the League Cup to hope for, which, thankfully, proved to be a thrilling and successful competition, ending with an equally thrilling and successful 2-1 victory for Rangers over Celtic, both goals scored by Jim Forrest – who was having an absolutely cracking League Cup competition, by the way, and scored in every round except the 1st leg of the St. Mirren games, which ended 0-0. En route, he scored two hat-tricks and belted four past St. Johnstone. Unstoppable.

Celtic were also dispensed with the following season in the Scottish Cup when right back Kai Johansen smashed the ball into the back of the Celtic net on the 70th minute as the Rangers fans erupted with joy.

JOHN GREIG
GLASGOW RANGERS & SCOTLAND

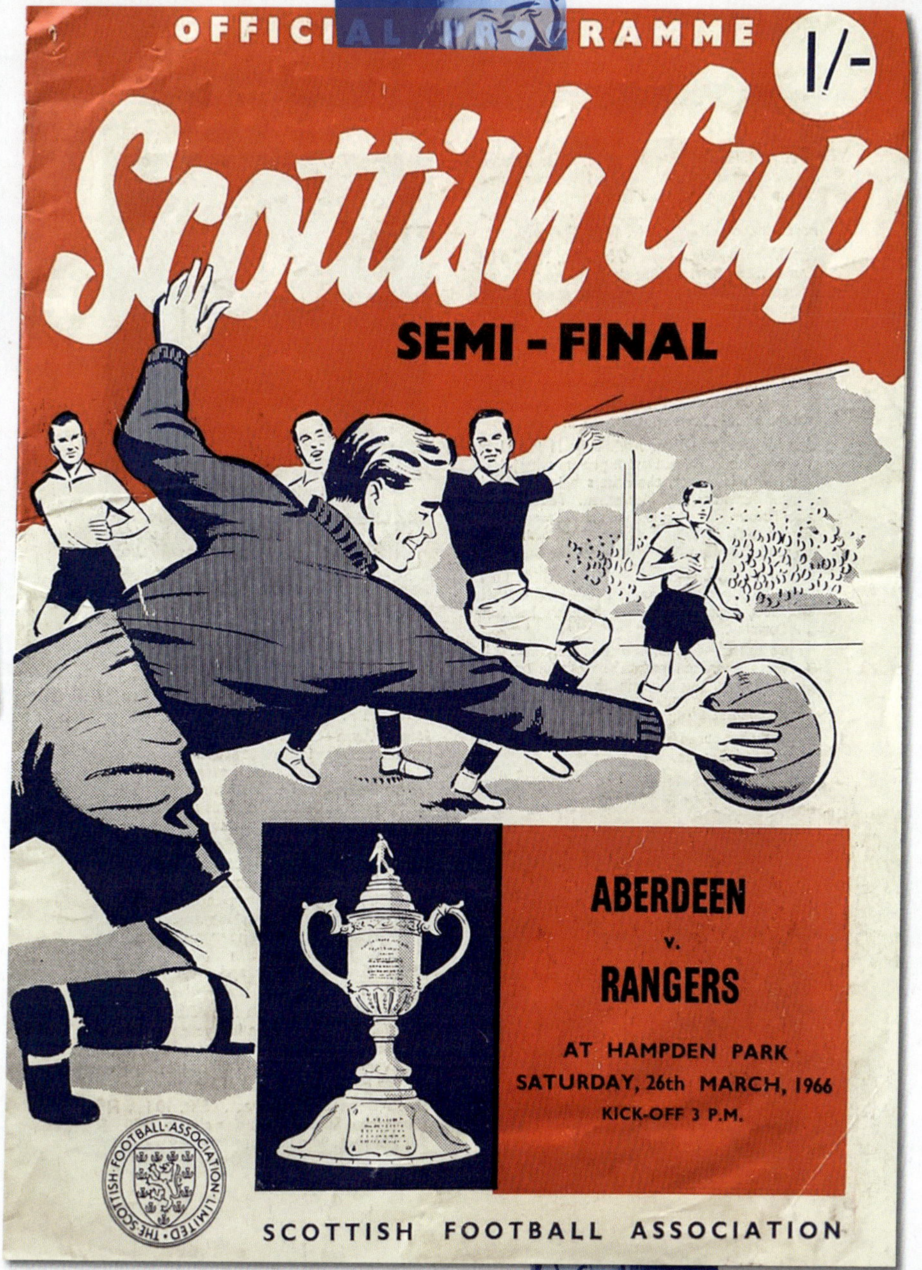

OFFICIAL PROGRAMME 1/-

Scottish Cup
SEMI - FINAL

ABERDEEN v. RANGERS

AT HAMPDEN PARK
SATURDAY, 26th MARCH, 1966
KICK-OFF 3 P.M.

SCOTTISH FOOTBALL ASSOCIATION

INTER-CITIES FAIRS CUP SEMI FINAL, 1ST LEG, FOOTBALL MATCH AT IBROX STADIUM, WEDNESDAY 14TH MAY 1969

YEARS

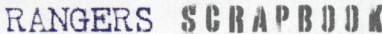

The end of that otherwise disappointing season also brought an end to Jim Baxter's career with Rangers and he left to play in Sunderland, England. It wasn't the last that Rangers fans would see of this outstanding player, for he would return for one season in 1969-70, but he would never again reach the heights that had delighted Rangers fans so much.

The low point for Rangers was reached when they were defeated in the first round of the Scottish Cup by Berwick Rangers. The date to be forgotten was the 27th of January 1967 and the Second Division club left the field victorious, 1-0. This humbling of mighty Rangers was symbolic of the instability that had managed to thread itself through club management and players in those difficult years.

Amidst this tremulous instability, those bleak years found another victim; Scot Symon. Fans had become increasingly dissatisfied with what they perceived

THE DOG-EARED YEARS

as a lack of direction in what was considered by some to be his old-fashioned management style, and following a 0-0 draw on the 28th of October 1967 against Dunfermline, Scot Symon left Ibrox and his 13-year career behind him. The hot seat was then inhabited by David White from Clyde. Sadly, Rangers proved a shirt too large for his slim experience.

Rangers were not spared tragedy either. On the 2nd of January 1971, at the end of a frustrating Old Firm game which had ended in a 1-1 draw, fans made their way to the exits, and on one of the

MAGNIFICENT 'TEAM'!

stairways the mass of fans suddenly began to crush those already on the stairs. The result was the deaths of 66 people; the cause was identified, as far as possible, and attributed to one of the fans tripping and falling on the stairs. Later, chairman Alastair Johnston would write: "The Ibrox Disaster is something that will never go away and neither should it. We know every one of these people who passed away or were injured were Rangers fans. They were all part of the family…"

Later, in a wonderful display of unity, Rangers and Celtic players joined forces against a Scottish XI to play a game for the Ibrox disaster fund.

Two more Scottish Cups would come Rangers' way during those lean years and another League Cup. But without doubt, the shining pinnacle of that period and indeed, in Rangers' history, came in 1972 with a Rangers' victory in the European Cup Winners' Cup. The game brought to an end five seasons in which Rangers had won no silverware except for the League Cup the previous season. And again, fans had the pleasure of watching Celtic go down, to a Derek Johnstone goal this time, which was all that was needed to do the damage. It was a much-needed boost to confidence in this era in which Rangers struggled to match the new found confidence of Celtic under their legendary manager Jock Stein. And as Celtic had already won the European Cup, the pressure was on when Rangers battled through to the final of the European Cup Winners Cup in 1972.

That season of 1971-72, was the third in which Colin Stein became top goalscorer for the club, and he struck again to score the opening goal in the final, which Rangers had reached after defeating another legendary club, Bayern Munich, 2-0 in the second leg of the semi-final.

Facing Dynamo Moscow, and armed only with pictures of the Russian players so that the team at least knew what the opposition players would look like, it was Colin Stein who charged forward towards the Russian goal on the 24th minute just able to shake off his Russian shadow. But with a perfectly weighted pass from Dave Smith, Stein contacted the ball superbly at full pace before thundering to the ground as the ball zipped into the top corner of the

CELTIC'S BOBBY MURDOCH (RIGHT) IS SHADOWED BY ALEX MACDONALD OF RANGERS, 1971

Dynamo net. Another extraordinary Rangers' moment for fans to savour forever. And cue for an invasion of the pitch by some of the 16,000 Rangers supporters.

But there was more jam to come, for just five minutes before half time, Smith was back up to his tricks again as he turned on the ball and sent over another beautiful cross straight to Johnston, who sailed into the air above the defenders to meet and gently slip the ball into the corner of the goal for number two.

Number three came in the first minute of the second half, a rather odd affair when Rangers goalie Peter McCloy floated the ball down the field so far that the Dynamo players seem to be bemused by it, leaving Willie Johnston

THE DOG-EARED YEARS

RANGERS FANS WATCH A SCOTTISH FA CUP MATCH, AGAINST ABERDEEN, IBROX, GLASGOW, 6TH MARCH 1971

RANGERS SCRAPBOOK

GLASGOW RANGERS' DEREK PARLANE CHALLENGES FOR THE BALL WITH JIM BROGAN OF CELTIC, 1973

to pick up the loose ball and push it past the Dynamo keeper.

That seemed to be it... Except that it wasn't. Rangers' energy seem to flag allowing the Russians to get back into the game and fans' nerves to shred, but as the final whistle blew to release extraordinary scenes and celebrations the likes of which even Rangers fans would find exceptional, the final scoreline read, Rangers 3 Dynamo Moscow 2.

For one man in particular, it was a truly deserved joyous culmination of years of hard work; Rangers' captain John

THE DOG-EARED YEARS

STADIUM AM BOEKELBERG, BORUSSIA MOENCHENGLADBACH V GLASGOW RANGERS, 24 OCTOBER, 1973

Greig had worked tirelessly through those difficult years before experiencing this truly exhilarating pinnacle of his career. It was unfortunate that Rangers fans invaded the pitch, understandably, as soon as the final whistle blew and the invasion descended into a nasty confrontation with the Spanish militia. This meant that the trophy was handed to captain John Greig unnoticed in the depths of Barcelona' Camp Nou Stadium, a rather melancholy, damp squib ending to a wonderful night.

And the heroes of that unforgettable match: Peter McCloy, Sandy Jardine, Willie Mathieson, John Greig, Derek Johnstone, David Smith, Tommy McLean, Alfie Conn, Colin Stein, Alex MacDonald, Willie Johnston. Rangers would not see another European final until the UEFA Cup of the 14th of May 2008.

THAT MAN

JOCK WALLACE 1975

That man. Now came the era of Jock Wallace as coach of Rangers serving with manager Willie Waddell. In tandem, they had steered the team to that thrilling Rangers' victory in the European Cup Winner's Cup final. After that, Waddell knew which way the wind was blowing, or should be blowing, and gave up his managerial seat to slip into a backroom role leaving Wallace to be appointed as manager, a position he retained until 1978. Under his guidance, Rangers rose again in stature, finally dethroned Celtic and won the League Championship again in 1974-75 after eleven years.

Rangers had delivered a season of cracking football in 1974-75 in which Kilmarnock were hammered 6-0, Dunfermline Athletic crushed 6-1, Motherwell knocked out 5-0 and Dumbarton flattened 5-1. Even Celtic didn't know what had had hit them and went down 2-1 and then 3-0 at Ibrox. Delicious moments to savour, with Sandy Jardine, Derek Johnstone, Tommy McLean and Derek Parlane lashing in the goals, unbeatable, with Parlane and Johnstone particularly consistent scorers and Parlane taking the top goalscorer honours. It was Johnstone, McLean and Parlane who had demolished Celtic. Not forgetting Greig, how could we, who dominated the centre field and swallowed every Celtic move he could possibly get a foot to.

For the first goal against Celtic, McLean had sent the most beautiful lofting ball into the penalty area for Johnstone to rise and put the ball away. Five minutes into the second half and MacDonald sent a great pass to McLean, who fired home Rangers' second. Parlane got into the act with just 15 minutes left to play, heading in Rangers' third. Glorious football.

The Gers lost just three games in the league, including the last one, 1-0 against Airdrieonians, who had also beaten them 3-4 earlier in the season (and only finished 11th in the table); but by then it no longer mattered, the evil spell had been broken and Rangers were a force to be reckoned with once more.

THE 1975 GLASGOW CUP FINAL BETWEEN RANGERS AND CELTIC AT HAMPDEN PARK ON THE 10TH OF MAY, 1975

JOCK WALLACE

RANGERS SCRAPBOOK

Throughout most of the 1970s, it was a rare occasion when Rangers finished a season without more silverware. It happened just three times in fact; 1972-73, 1976-77 and 1979-80. The Light Blues compensated for those disappointments by treating fans to another two domestic trebles and one double. Such astounding achievements, but for Rangers seeming almost commonplace!

The second of those trebles came in 1977-78 in a season that started off with two defeats in the league competition, ended with a 2-1 victory over Aberdeen in the Scottish

DEREK JOHNSTONE IN ACTION FOR RANGERS, 1978

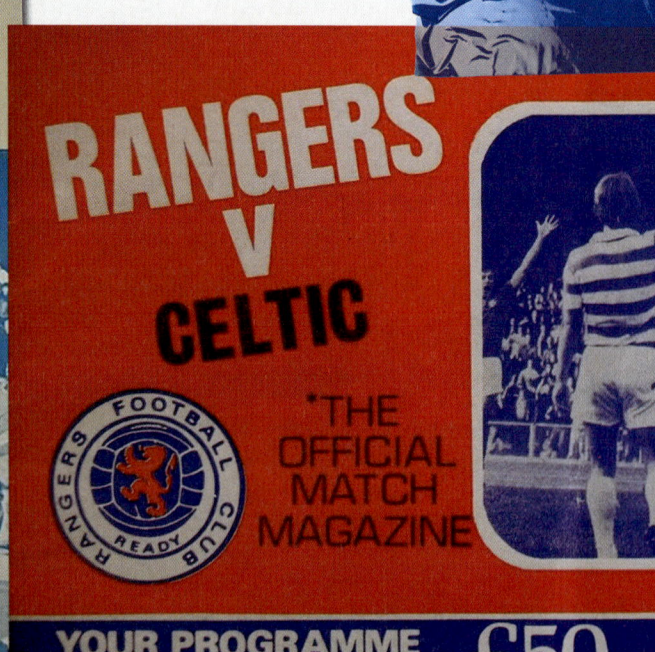

THAT MAN JOCK WALLACE

DEREK PARLANE IN ACTION FOR RANGERS, 1978

Cup and included a delightful 2-1 victory over Celtic in the League Cup. It was sweet revenge over a powerful Aberdeen side that had dogged them all season and beaten them 3-1 and 3-0 in the league; which was why fans' hearts had been racing when the Light Blues lost to Celtic in the league late in March 1978, 0-2. The title hung in the balance. But Wallace had gathered a team that still boasted such greats as Sandy Jardine, Derek Johnstone and John Greig and that magnificent man between the posts, Peter McCloy, so Aberdeen were left in second place with 53 points to Rangers' 55.

When Willie Waddell decided to vacate his managerial seat, he turned his talents to bringing the stadium up-to-date, paying special attention to the safety features, the tragedy of a short time before still burned into his memory.

It took many years and began when the Derry stand was filled with benches and renamed the Centenary Stand. Only in 1977 was planning permission granted that entailed demolishing three sides of the old stadium and erecting three

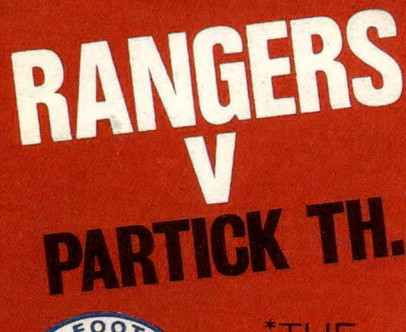

RANGERS SCRAPBOOK

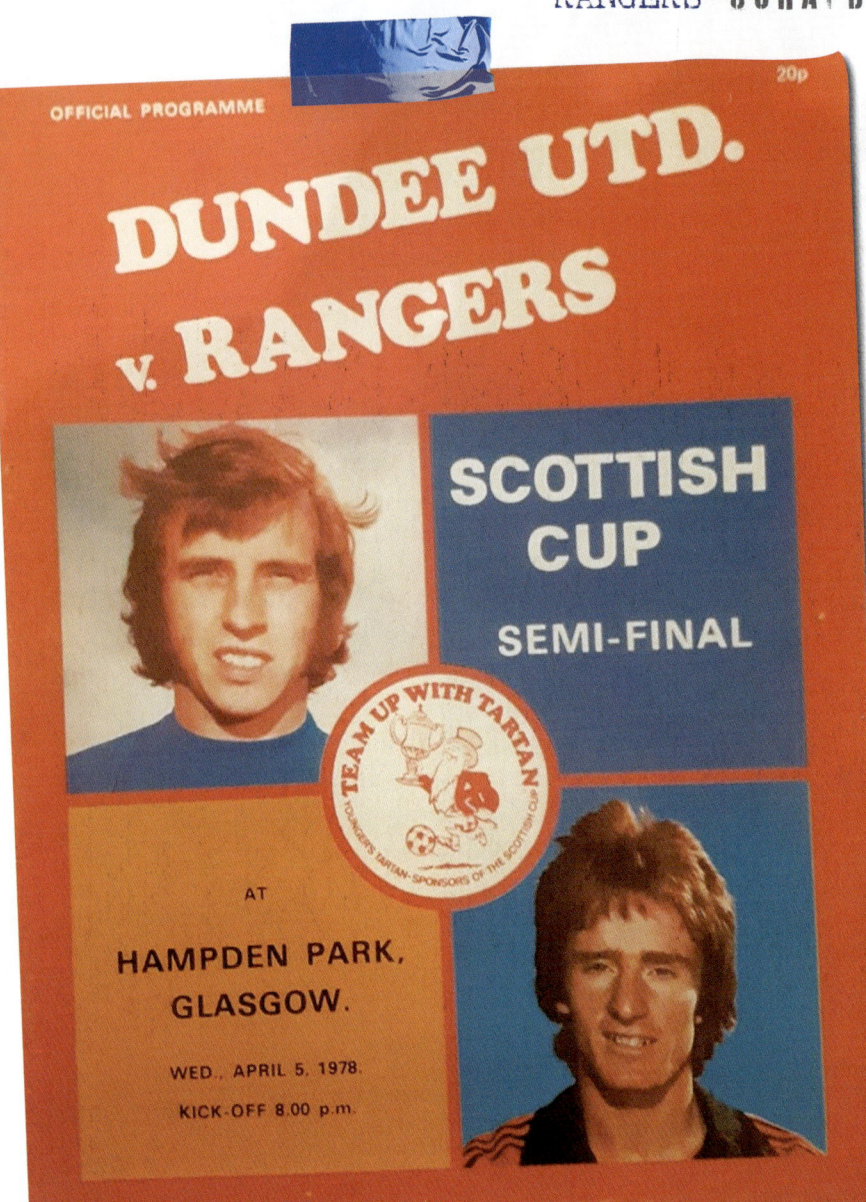

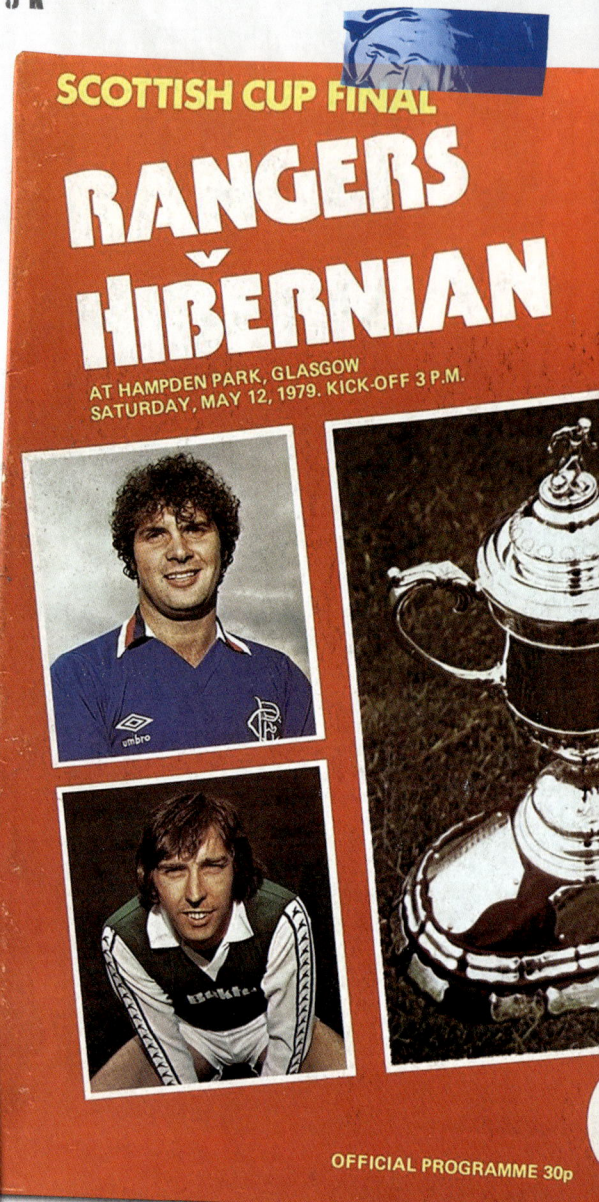

GLASGOW HERALD Monday March 19 1979

Thistle provide ideal warm-up

THAT MAN JOCK WALLACE

new stands. In 1979, the 'Rangers end' of the stadium, the Copeland Road Stand, was opened, and in 1980 the Broomloan Road Stand, sometimes referred to as the 'Celtic end', was completed, followed one year later by a larger stand in place of the Derry, which was renamed the Goven stand.

And so Rangers and the 1970s parted company. It was a very peculiar final season of the decade for the Light Blues. They finished fifth in the table having lost an astonishing 14 games. They only won five of the first 15 games, a league season to wipe from memory as quickly as possible. And the Scottish Cup run ended in a disaster with a defeat to Celtic and in the League Cup competition they were booted out in round three with two defeats to Aberdeen 1-3 and 0-2.

What would the 1980s hold in store.

LEAGUE CUP FINAL ABERDEEN V RANGERS HAMPDEN - GLASGOW. COLIN JACKSON (3RD LEFT) IS CONGRATULATED BY DEREK JOHNSTONE (4), DEREK PARLANE, ALEX MACDONALD (6), GORDON SMITH AND BOBBY RUSSELL AFTER SCORING THE WINNER FOR RANGERS 1979

THE LEAGUE CUP BELONGS TO RANGERS

John Greig had ended his playing career in May 1978 when Jock Wallace departed, and taken over the team management. He'd managed to bring the Scottish and League Cups back to Rangers, perhaps on the fumes of Wallace's achievements as the teams were identical. But that last season of the 1970s, Greig's first full season as manager, had been a washout, so all eyes were now ferociously fixed on him.

Anyone hoping for a decade of treble victories, was going to be severely disappointed. In fact, it took until the middle of the new decade (the 1986-87 season to be precise), by which time Rangers had limped home in fifth place in the league competition, before they rallied and won another Division One Championship.

Let's start with the good news; 1980-81 season brought the - always longed-for - Scottish Cup Back to Ibrox. Following a 0-0 draw, the replay saw the Light Blues take off the gloves and dissect their opponents, Dundee United, 4-1... which, having beaten them twice in the league was the least that a Rangers fan could expect.

Dundee were dangerous opponents as the replay got under way, though, with Bannon always threatening, pressurising the Gers, and a blistering free kick almost put Rangers on the back foot, but it whistled just wide of goalkeeper Jim Stewart's airborne body. It wasn't the last time Stewart would show his calibre. But Rangers

1981 LEAGUE CUP FINAL RANGERS V DUNDEE UTD (2-1). HAMPDEN - GLASGOW. RANGERS DEFENDER ALEX MILLER BATTLES TO CLEAR THE BALL

1980 SCOTTISH FA CUP FINAL, CELTIC V GLASGOW RANGERS, BOBBY RUSSELL TAKES THE BALL FROM FRANK MCGARVEY

RANGERS SCRAPBOOK

JOHN MCCLELLAND RECEIVES HIS MEDAL AND THE LEAGUE CUP TROPHY FROM JIM FARRY, 25 MARCH, 1984

showed what they were made of with a razor-sharp counter attack just seconds later showing that thrills for the fans were assured.

Then Rangers were back in the Dundee half, and a Johnstone flick through the defenders found Cooper free to chip the ball over the goalkeeper before it, agonisingly slowly, dribbled into the net. That signalled the end of Rangers the nice guys. Cooper sent in a viciously swerving, beautiful free-kick, which was volleyed in mercilessly by Russell for number two. A fabulous goal just after twenty minutes had passed.

Only for United's Dodds to score after that man Bannon had pushed the ball into the penalty area two minutes later.

Now the fight for the ball became intense, but Ranger's class was obvious, Johnstone and McDonald only thwarted by the keeper after a glorious move. And McDonald was lurking again following a superb through pass by Cooper, to wrong-foot the defence and push a one-touch strike into the net. This was Rangers' play at its finest.

Chances came and went unclaimed for both sides though only the Dundee bar prevented another Rangers' goal. But just to make sure, McDonald found another huge space and when a long pass dropped in front of him, he held off the defender's challenge and slid the ball away into the net past the Dundee keeper.

The game had been a display of superb football by Rangers and they well deserved the 4-1 victory in their 24th Scottish Cup and the silverware at the end. Unexpectedly, it also proved to be the last Scottish Cup for the club until 1992.

John McDonald was top goalscorer for the following two seasons at Rangers and scored in five of the matches that won Rangers the League Cup in November 1981, against Dundee United once more, victory achieved with a 2-1 win. That

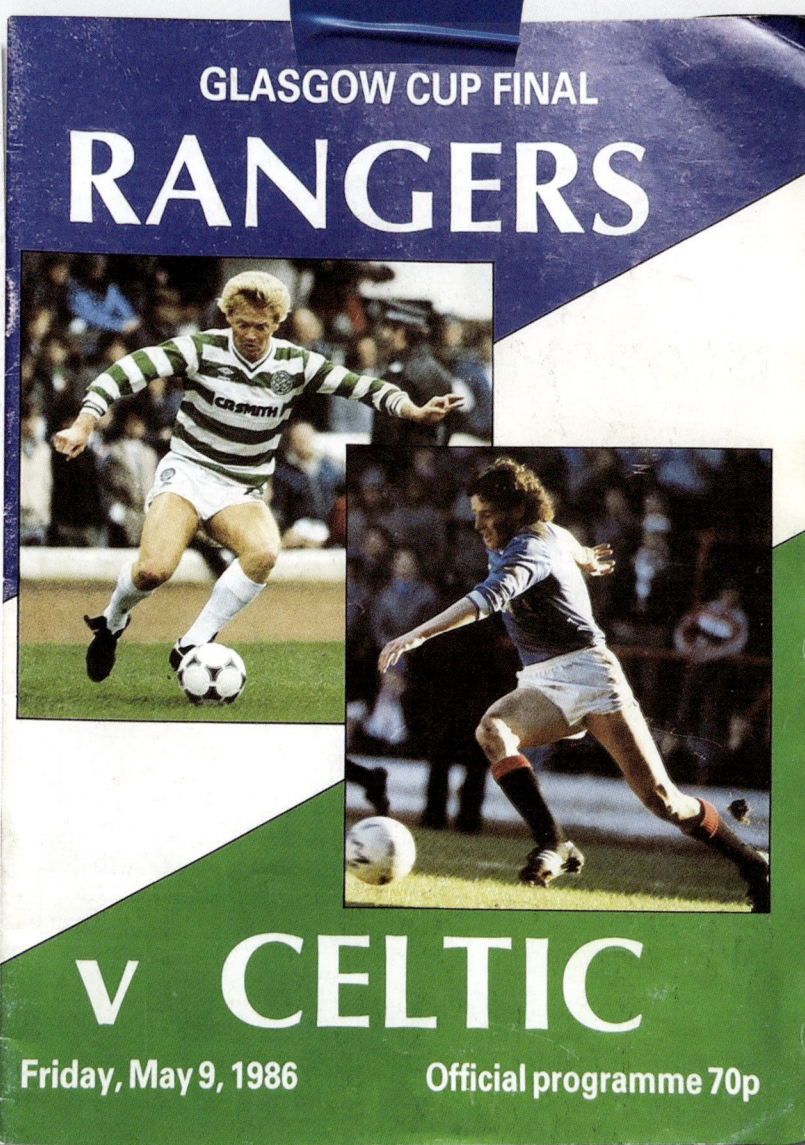

League Cup win was the first of six that Rangers would achieve in the 1980s, three of them back to back in 1986, 1987, and 1988. The first of that triplet of League Cups coincided with the first league title win – since 1975 the league had been named the Scottish Premier Division – for 10 years, and those two honours also gave Rangers the first of two doubles that decade.

There were other notable moments off the field, too. In the 1985-86 season, the managers' revolving-door season, four managers came and went: Jock Wallace, ending his second spell as manager, (which had started in 1983), until the 7th of April, Alex Totten until the

RANGERS SCRAPBOOK

THE LEAGUE CUP BELONGS TO RANGERS

MCNINN (LEFT) ALLY MCCOIST (RIGHT) AND TERRY BUTCHER (RIGHT) ALL OF RANGERS CELEBRATE WITH THE SKOL CUP TROPHY AFTER THE FINAL AGAINST CELTIC IN SCOTLAND. RANGERS WON THE MATCH 2-1, 1986

16th of April, John Mackay until the 1st of May, and then finally stability arriving with Graeme Souness on May 1st, Souness rewarding his appointment with the league title in 1986-87, the first for Rangers in nine years.

The wonderful Peter McCloy, whose number of appearances had diminished in his final years at the club, departed Ibrox that season as well, after 451 outings for the Light Blues. A magnificent 16-year career.

As the decade drew to a close - we should call it Ally McCoist's decade, for he achieved a remarkable top goalscorer spot eight times, five of those back to back, and nine League Championships in total - and a new one arrived, Rangers won the Scottish Premier Division title for the second successive season.

How could anyone know that in the decade now lounging around the corner of 1990-91, Rangers would rise higher than the most passionate fans could have imagined, to complete what can only be called a decade beyond compare.

DOUBLES & TREBLES

Rangers hurled themselves into the 1990s having launched a run of league title wins – the league had been renamed yet again and was now the Premier Division – that would eventually bring them nine championships. They would lose just one title race between 1990 and the year 2000. It was galling that the team that stopped them from achieving the clean ten was Celtic, but the highlights for Rangers were too great to be diminished by that detail.

Souness had greeted the new year with a daring signing; Maurice Johnston was a former Celtic player, and many in the Rangers' department of the Old Firm were not happy. But a taboo had been broken, and during his two-year stint with the club Johnston proved that he was prepared to play his heart out for Rangers, too, and as top goalscorer in the 1990-91 season as well, helping his team to gain two Scottish league titles with 46 goals in 100 matches. The new manager would also oversee the English invasion that saw players such as (infamous) centre back and captain Terry Butcher (dropped after he was, in part, to blame for the 2–1 defeat against Dundee United in September 1990), full-back Gary Stevens, goalkeeper Chris Woods, midfielder Trevor Steven and forward Mark Hateley lending their talents to the Scottish camp.

Johnston's first season, by the way, saw Rangers begin with an uncharacteristic stumble as they lost the first two games and drew the third one against Celtic. After eight matches they had only won two of them, causing more than a deal of agitation amongst fans before they pulled themselves together, then wobbling again in February and March 1990 as they put together four draws and a loss, after which they whacked Celtic off the pitch with a 3-0 win, finally clinching the title by a comfortable 51 points to 2nd-placed Aberdeen's 44.

JOHN COLLINS (CENTRE) OF CELTIC IS CHALLENGED BY TERRY HURLOCK (RIGHT) OF RANGERS DURING THE SKOL CUP FINAL AT HAMPDEN PARK IN GLASGOW, 01 OCTOBER, 1990

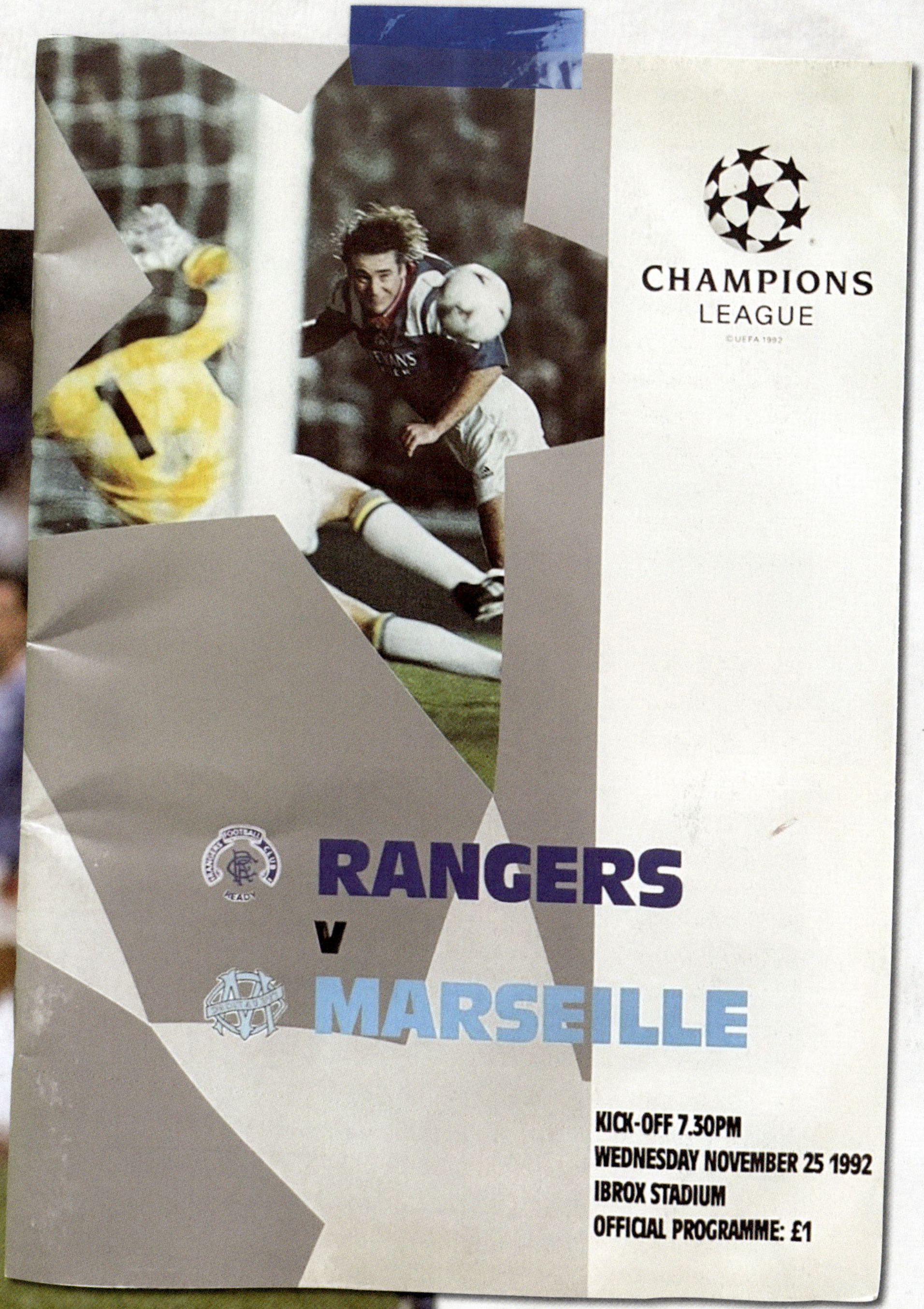

A glance at the table for the 1990s shows that Rangers were almost invincible for much of the time, with the exception of 1997-98 the final unfortunate year of Walter Smith's tenure as manager, a season in which the lads had nothing to show for all their efforts. 12 years had passed since the club last finished without a trophy. Several legendary and long-serving players also called time on their Ranger's careers that year, amongst them were Stuart McCall, Ally McCoist, Andy Goram and Ian Durrant. But upon his departure, Smith

GALORE!

Ally McCoist (L) and Maurice Johnston celebrate after Rangers had beaten Aberdeen in the title decider 2-0, to claim the 1990/91 Scottish Premier Division title at Ibrox on May 11, 1991

left behind a trail of silver that stretched all the way back to Graeme Souness' own parting of the ways in 1991. (The year in which Ukrainian midfielder Oleksiy Oleksandrovych Mykhaylychenko joined the Rangers' ranks, by the way, and would score 20 goals in 110 appearances for the club over the course of the next five years.)

A summary of the Gers' achievements between the 1990-91 and 1999-00 is as follows: five doubles, two trebles, nine Premier Division titles, five Scottish Cups, five League Cups. There were two back-to-back doubles, 1991 and 1992, immediately followed by a triple in 1993, an out-of-this-world achievement by Rangers. That 1992 victory in the Scottish Cup Final when they beat Airdrieonians 2-1 having dispensed with Celtic in the semi-final 1-0, was their first win in the competition since 1981.

They enjoyed the experience so much that they repeated it the following year in 1993 when they beat Aberdeen by the same margin, 2-1. Aberdeen had been chasing Rangers all year to no avail, because Rangers had dominated the season, and not only did they beat Aberdeen in the Scottish Cup, they also beat them to the top of the Premier League with 73 points to 64, but they had, by that time, already snatched the League Cup from them by beating them 2-1 in the final of that competition, too. Rangers had claimed their fifth domestic treble.

DOUBLES AND TREBLES GALORE!

The indomitable Ally McCoist clocked up his most successful season ever, becoming top goalscorer for the last time with 49 goals to his credit. Let's quickly pay tribute to his talent by mentioning his final (almost) hat-trick for Rangers in the semi-final of the League Cup against St Johnstone. Goram saved Ranger's blushes more than once with terrific goalkeeping as both teams fought hard for dominance, until the 24th minute when McCoist found a huge gap, did a wonderful swivel in front of the St. Johnstone goal and whipped the ball in for number one. The second was in fact an own goal, but McCoist was harrying McGowne so intensely that the St. Johnstone defender was forced into the blunder with help from McCoist's right foot. Then in the second half, Rangers powered forward and with 68 minutes played, McCoist was sent through the defence after a lofting pass and neatly avoiding the lunging legs of McGinnis he tucked the ball away past the approaching keeper, Rhodes.

St. Johnstone managed to put one away before the end, but the glory belonged to magnificent McCoist and the Rangers lads.

Worth mentioning: 1995 heralded the end of one of the most wonderful partnerships that Rangers fans had ever had the pleasure of witnessing when Mark Hateley left the club bringing to a close his thrilling football exchanges with Ally McCoist.

And then more talent arrived the following year, 1966, in the shape of a player that Rangers fans dubbed The Hammer. Jörg Albertz brought his mighty long-range drives into service for the club for which the fans would always be grateful and which earned the midfielder a lasting place in their hearts. Not least for firing the most extraordinary free-kick at the speed of

RANGERS WIN THE SCOTTISH PREMIER DIVISION LEAGUE CHAMPIONSHIP AFTER VICTORY OVER DUNDEE UNITED AT IBROX IN GLASGOW, SCOTLAND, 8 MAY 1993

light past the Celtic lineup and into the Celtic net in January 1997. Rangers took a 3-1 victory from that encounter. With the arrival of manager Dick Advocaat, however, Albertz often found himself out of favour, although he still managed to gain league championship medals in 1999 and 2000.

And then one quick stop before skipping over the dreadful season of 1997-98 when no silverware gleamed anywhere, and Rangers parted company with one of their finest, if most erratic, players at the end of the season. On the 26th of March 1998 Paul Gascoigne was sold to English club Middlesborough having made little impact throughout the year. He'd only made 74 appearances since joining the club in 1995 but managed 30 goals, his highest tally for any club.

He had a successful first season scoring 19 goals, not far behind top goalscorer Gordon Drurie who had 23. And who can forget that Old Firm contest when he galloped almost the length of the pitch to outrun the Celtic defenders and pick up on a superb pass to score against Celtic at Celtic Park. Stunning football savvy. And then his hat-trick against Aberdeen on the 28th of April 1996 in the league. He was rewarded by being named PFA Scotland Players' Player of the Year and SFWA Footballer of the Year.

During his second season, Gascoigne was already suffering from his alcohol problem, though he helped the Gers take the Scottish League Cup from Hearts 4-3 in the final, scoring twice,

DOUBLES AND TREBLES GALORE!

RANGERS STRIKER ALLY MCCOIST CLASHES WITH PETER GRANT AS PAUL GASCOIGNE (LEFT) AND CHARLIE MILLER LOOK ON. 19 SEPTEMBER, 1995

although by the end of the 1997-98 season it was clear that all was not well with the star player whose star was rapidly fading, and after 3 goals in 28 games, the dream was over for Gascoigne and for Rangers.

There was another triple to enjoy in the 1998-99 season – the first in six years and Rangers' sixth – the season when Walter Smith departed to allow Dutchman Dick Advocaat to take over the club's fate. His appointment was, in the eyes of many, to have far reaching consequences years later for the club. In this year of magnificent results, no one could have imagined it ending the way it did. Especially as Rangers started off the league competition by losing to Heart of Midlothian 2-1. And, painfully, received the worst hiding from Celtic that they could possibly have had, going down 5-1 to their arch rivals; then claiming the Scottish Cup against, yes, Celtic, 1-0 in the final. The Gers then swooped home in the league (now having undergone another identity change and

RANGERS SCRAPBOOK

PAUL GASCOIGNE (LEFT) AND TEAMMATE ALLY MCCOIST POSE WITH THE TROPHY AFTER THE SCOTTISH COCA COLA CUP FINAL BETWEEN RANGERS AND HEARTS AT CELTIC PARK IN GLASGOW, 18 NOV 1996

called the Scottish Premier League, having broken with the Scottish Football League) ahead of, guess who, yes, Celtic again, with 77 to 71 points.

It had been a fight to the finish with the Glasgow rivals that Rangers finally decided in their favour just three games before the season ended. On the 2nd of May 1999 the two sides met, and with tension to cut with a knife, the fouls weren't long in coming. But Rangers kept their heads and not allowing themselves to be distracted had netted the first goal after just twelve minutes when a flowing Rangers' move ended via van Bronckhorst and then Wallace, who had sprinted in behind the defence and sent the ball airborne right in front of McCann, who struck it once in the air; in it went. Heaven.

With Celtic beginning to panic, the referee was struck by a flying missile from the crowd after forty minutes had passed and was seen on the ground with blood pouring from his head. And when Rangers were awarded a penalty fans invaded the pitch.

It was a touch-and-go penalty decision, but Albertz had no hesitation in putting it away with his left foot to extend the lead to 2-0.

Controversy flared again when Celtic keeper Kerr handled outside his penalty area and given a yellow card instead of being dismissed. But McCann was there again to see justice done. On the 76th minute, with the Celtic defence split, he skipped past

DOUBLES AND TREBLES GALORE!

four games and then beaten St. Johnstone in the final 2-1 on November the 29th 1998.

Dick Advocaat had seen the need to replace the aging Rangers' stars and brought in a raft of new players such as midfielder Giovanni van Bronckhorst, left-winger Neil McCann, full back Arthur Numan and striker Rod Wallace, top goalscorer for two successive seasons. Goram's replacement was Lionel Charbonnier, and winger Andrei Kanchelskis was a £5.5 million part of the twenty-five million pounds that Advocaat would splash out that summer. Several of the new signings were less successful and lasted but a few seasons, forward Gabriel Amato for example or defenders Colin Hendry and Daniel Prodan (who played not one game). Advocaat had also handed Italian defender Lorenzo Pier Paolo Amoruso the captaincy of the Gers in 1998. Which proved to be a mixed blessing, as he was often booed by fans, lost the captaincy, and then engaged in an ongoing war of words with Advocaat. He was out of favour for long stretches until Alex McLeish arrived to take over the reigns from Advocaat. In midfield, Albertz, van Bronckhorst, Ferguson and Kanchelskis were solid in providing opportunities for the forwards as Adovcaat's new boys began to show their value.

It's worth mentioning an inspiring European game in a season in which Rangers did well in Europe, the match against Bayer Leverkusen in the UEFA Cup on the 22nd of October 1998.

It was van Bronckhorst who rushed forward into the space as the Bayer defence was split open, and holding off the defensive challenge kept his cool and slid in the first goal. Rangers split the defence wide open again as Wallace brought the ball down to the penalty area and with a deft pass across to Johansson gave the forward an almost open goal for number 2.

But there might have been even more than that as Rangers took the game to the Germans with style and bravura. This was the game that saw Barry Ferguson emerge to the stardom that would bring him the captaincy of the club between 2000 and 2003 and again between 2005 and 2009 and 45 outings in the Scottish national team, the first of which had also taken place in 1998. He also brought 'the Barry turn' to Ibrox, his 180-degree swivel. It was just such a turn that had presented van Bronckhorst with his goal opportunity. The Germans pulled one goal back in October, but Rangers went through to the next round after a home leg 1-1 draw. It was to be the best European run for the club in a long time.

his shadow and raced into space to dance around the Celtic keeper and seal the 3-0 win for Rangers, their 100th victory against Celtic. The lads to thank were: Klos, Porrini, Amoruso, Vidmar, Hendry, van Bronckhorst, Albertz, McCann, Reyna, Wallace, Amato. Subs: Niemi, McInnes, Johansson, Wilson and Riccio.

There were some other erratic results that season; beating Dundee United away from home 2-1 and losing to them 1-0 at home; crushing St. Johnstone 7-0 only to lose to them later in the season 3-1.

But, no worries, the League Cup had already fallen to them after they had conceded just one goal in

BELL'S PREMIER DIVISION. RANGERS V ST JOHNSTONE (2-1). IBROX - GLASGOW. BRIAN LAUDRUP CELEBRATES FOR RANGERS WITH MARCO NEGRI (BACK, RIGHT) IAN DURRANT (LEFT) AND JONAS THERN, 1998

DOUBLES AND TREBLES GALORE!

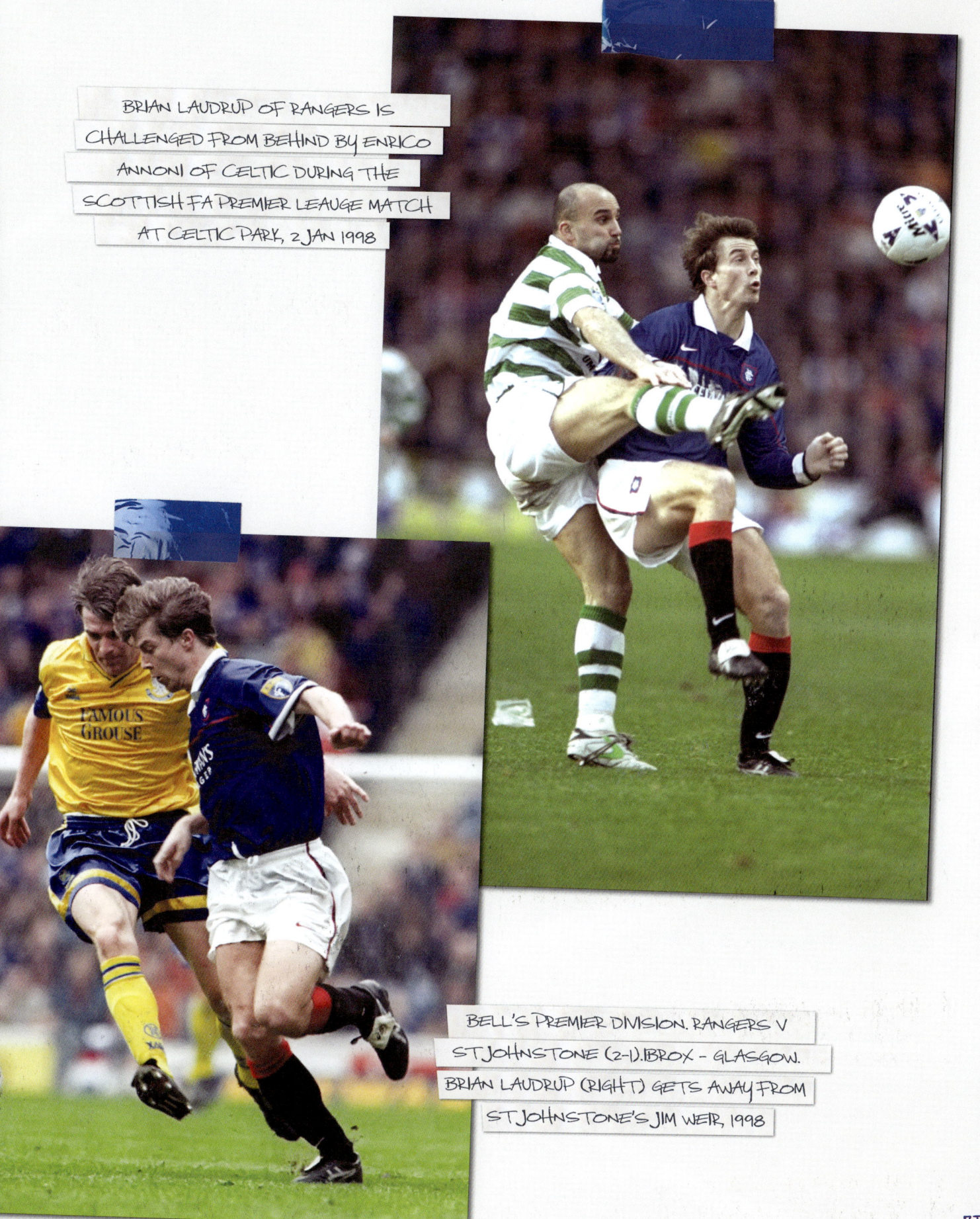

Brian Laudrup of Rangers is challenged from behind by Enrico Annoni of Celtic during the Scottish FA Premier League match at Celtic Park, 2 Jan 1998

Bell's Premier Division. Rangers v St Johnstone (2-1). Ibrox - Glasgow. Brian Laudrup (right) gets away from St Johnstone's Jim Weir, 1998

RANGERS SCRAPBOOK

Ranger's 120th season of competitive football came to an end in the year 2000 with yet another double; the league and the Scottish Cup fell to their skilled feet. On the heels of the triple the previous season, Rangers were truly in a class of their own. They only lost two matches in the league, against Dundee and Motherwell, romping home to the title by a record 21-point margin in May 2000 bringing a memorable season to a climax with their second-consecutive league title.

DOUBLES AND TREBLES GALORE!

It had been Aberdeen who were on their heels in the Scottish Cup and League Cup runs, though, and the two teams came away from the battles with one win apiece, Rangers falling to Aberdeen in the League Cup qualifying round 1-0, but wrenching the Scottish Cup from them in the final 4-0, a game in which the Aberdeen goalkeeper, Jim Leighton, sustained a serious head injury and was stretchered off.

As a welcome to the new millennium, Rangers had given fans a joyous run of 22-games without defeat as well as four games when they hammered home five goals and six when they scored four, plus a 6-2 thumping of Motherwell and a 7-1 dismantling of Dundee. It had been a decade of unparalleled achievement and glorious, riotously thrilling football. How could life get any better.

The answer; it didn't get much worse.

THE RANGERS PLAYERS CELEBRATE AFTER THE SCOTTISH F.A CUP FINAL AGAINST ABERDEEN AT HAMPDEN PARK, GLASGOW, SCOTLAND, 27 MAY 2000

SNAKES

In the 2000-01 season the lads took a breather from winning and allowed Celtic to slip in to claim the league title. Celtic also pushed them out of the League Cup competition and Dundee United did the same in the Scottish Cup. A season not to linger over, especially as Celtic had put six past them in the derby game in August 2000, yes, six, as the defence collapsed and Barry Ferguson was sent off. Revenge is sweet, however, and on the 26th of November 2000 it was Rangers turn to turn up the heat delivering a 5-1 hiding... before suffering two more defeats in the New Year.

What better way to get over the bumps in the pitch than to claim another double the following season; a season that would be without some well-loved players: Jörg Albertz, Sergio Porrini, Rod Wallace, Lionel Charbonnier or Giovanni van Bronckhorst, but see a new man at the helm. Alex McLeish took over when Advocaat resigned in December 2001 after a 1-1 draw against Hibernian, the last of a series of poor results that had included two losses to Celtic.

It was too late to salvage the league, and the title slipped away thanks to a resurgent Celtic team, but the Scottish Cup proved that Ranger's rivals were not invincible, as the Gers took the silver with a 3-2 victory. They had already secured the League Cup in March with a 4-0 win over plucky Ayr, who gave as good as they got until half-time approached when Tore Andre Flo slapped away the magnificent first goal from a steep angle and Barry Ferguson then hit home a penalty. Ranger's nerves settled after that and in the second half it was not long before the second pair of goals sent fans into uproar. Caniggia avoided a couple of defenders to volley the ball in and then got his head down low to head the ball just over the line to secure the win beyond doubt.

At last, with the 2002-03 season – sadly Tore André Flo had gone and Barry Ferguson would captain the successful side for the last time. The Scottish Football

CLAUDIO REYNA (LEFT) AND LORENZO AMORUSO BATTLES FOR AN AERIAL BALL WITH CELTIC STRIKER CHRIS SUTTON, 26 NOVEMBER 2000

SPL RANGERS V CELTIC. MIDFIELDER BARRY FERGUSON IS CHALLENGED BY STILIAN PETROV 26 MARCH 2000

& LADDERS

1. FC BOCHOLT
1900 E.V.
100 Jahre
RANGERS FOOTBALL CLUB READY
Nr. 2255
1. FC Bocholt
Glasgow Rangers
Mittwoch, 12. Juli,
Uhr, Am Hünting

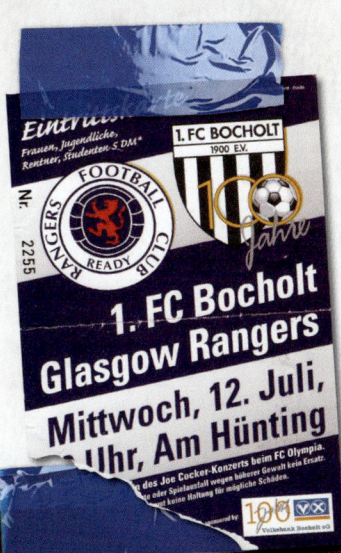

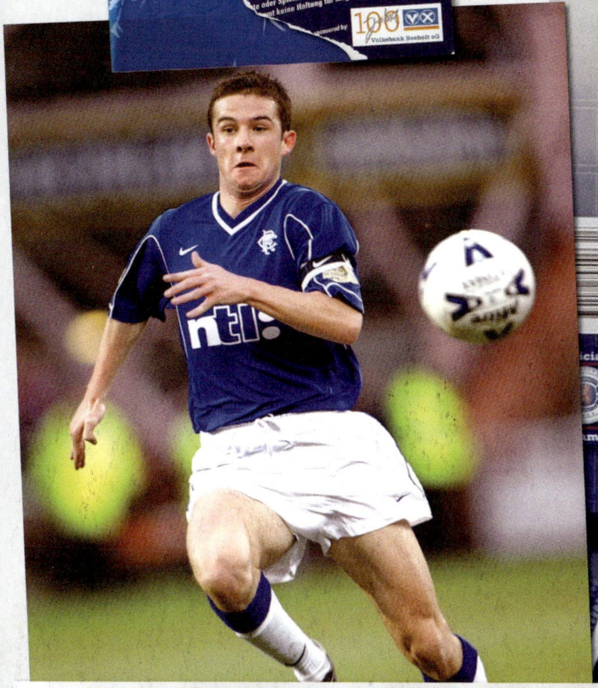

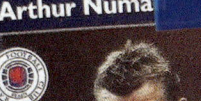

BARRY FERGUSON DURING THE SCOTTISH PREMIER DIVISION MATCH AGAINST HEARTS PLAYED AT TYNECASTLE, IN EDINBURGH, SCOTLAND, 3 DEC 2000

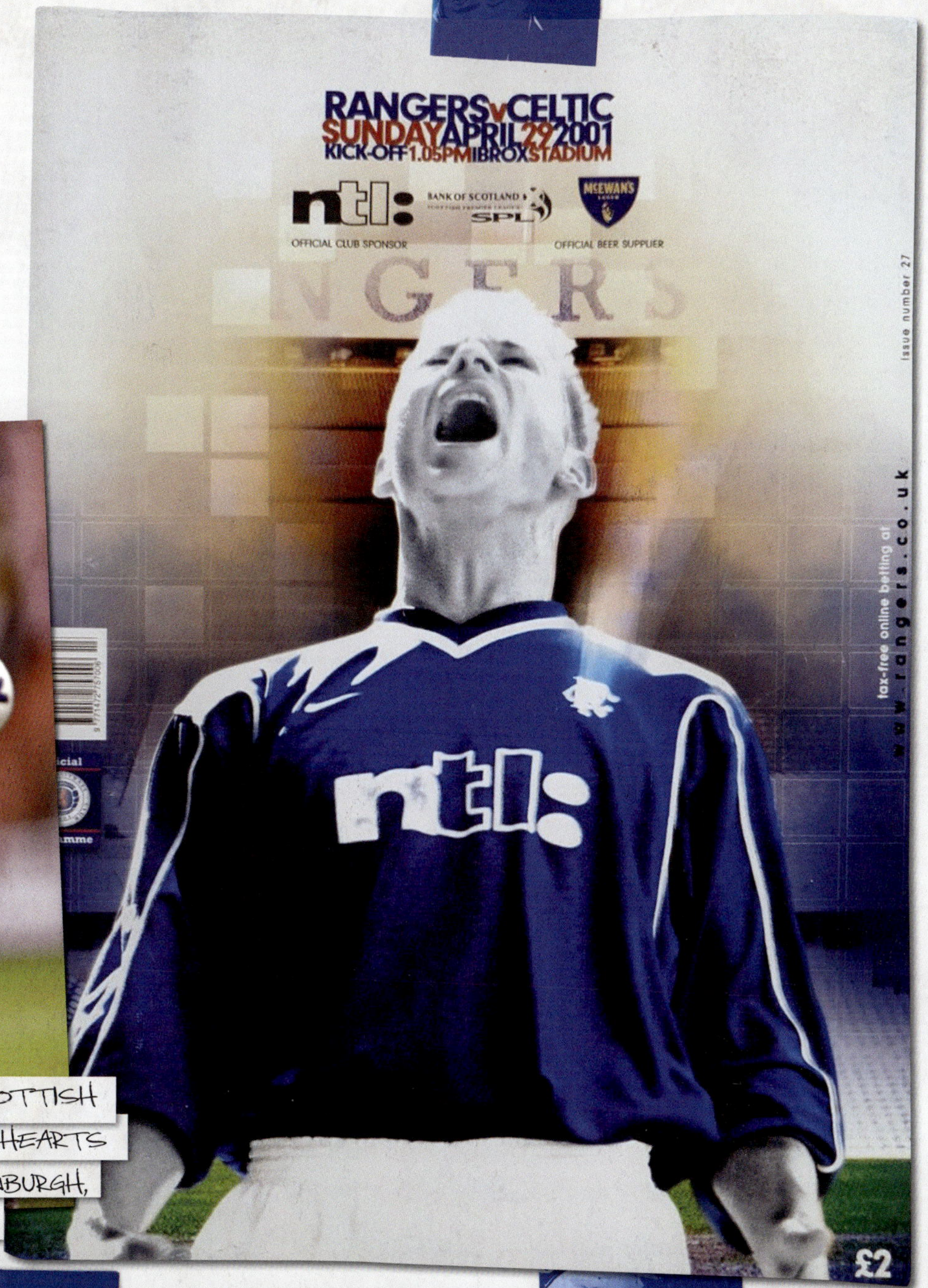

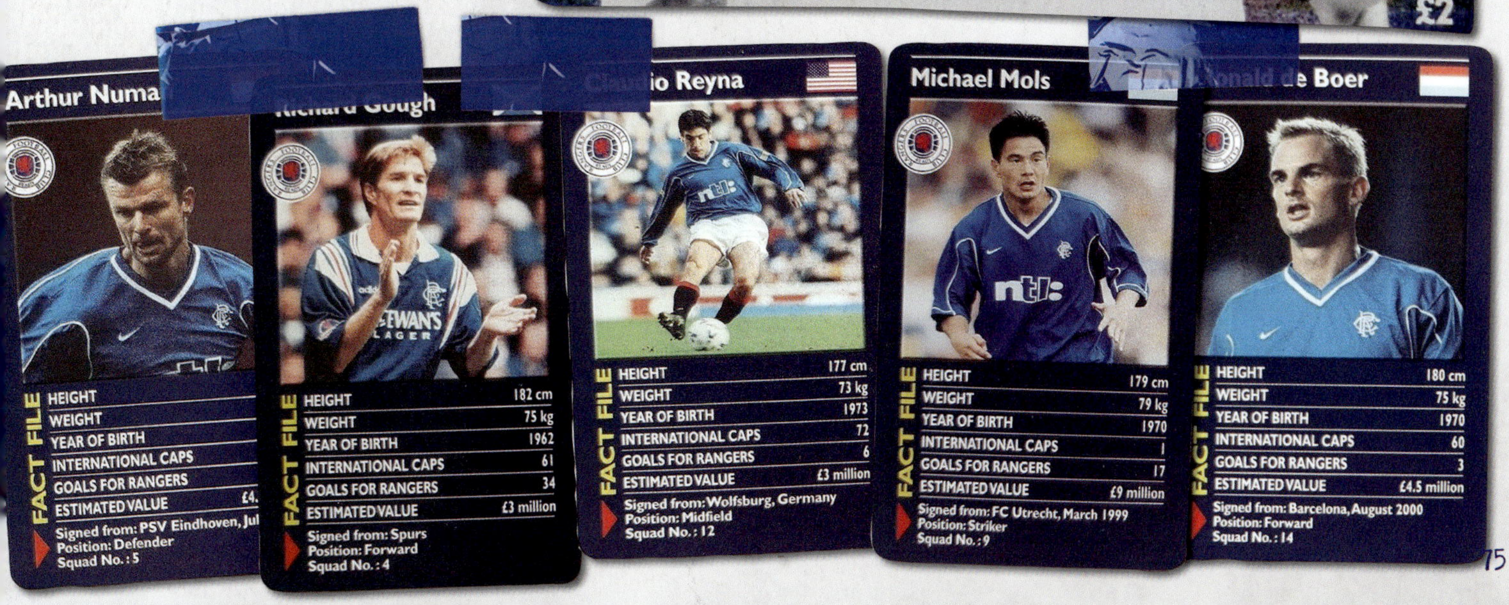

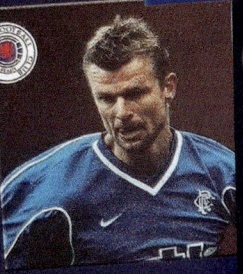

RANGERS v CELTIC
SUNDAY APRIL 29 2001
KICK-OFF 1.05PM IBROX STADIUM
ntl:
OFFICIAL CLUB SPONSOR
BANK OF SCOTLAND
SPL
McEWAN'S
OFFICIAL BEER SUPPLIER
issue number 27
tax-free online betting at
www.rangers.co.uk
£2

Arthur Numa
FACT FILE
HEIGHT
WEIGHT
YEAR OF BIRTH
INTERNATIONAL CAPS
GOALS FOR RANGERS
ESTIMATED VALUE £4.
Signed from: PSV Eindhoven, Jul
Position: Defender
Squad No.: 5
Richard Gough
FACT FILE
HEIGHT 182 cm
WEIGHT 75 kg
YEAR OF BIRTH 1962
INTERNATIONAL CAPS 61
GOALS FOR RANGERS 34
ESTIMATED VALUE £3 million
Signed from: Spurs
Position: Forward
Squad No.: 4
Claudio Reyna
FACT FILE
HEIGHT 177 cm
WEIGHT 73 kg
YEAR OF BIRTH 1973
INTERNATIONAL CAPS 72
GOALS FOR RANGERS 6
ESTIMATED VALUE £3 million
Signed from: Wolfsburg, Germany
Position: Midfield
Squad No.: 12
Michael Mols
FACT FILE
HEIGHT 179 cm
WEIGHT 79 kg
YEAR OF BIRTH 1970
INTERNATIONAL CAPS 1
GOALS FOR RANGERS 17
ESTIMATED VALUE £9 million
Signed from: FC Utrecht, March 1999
Position: Striker
Squad No.: 9
onald de Boer
FACT FILE
HEIGHT 180 cm
WEIGHT 75 kg
YEAR OF BIRTH 1970
INTERNATIONAL CAPS 60
GOALS FOR RANGERS 3
ESTIMATED VALUE £4.5 million
Signed from: Barcelona, August 2000
Position: Forward
Squad No.: 14

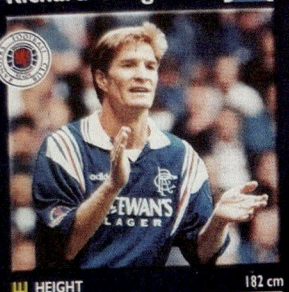

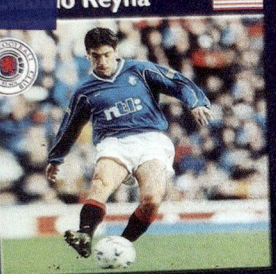

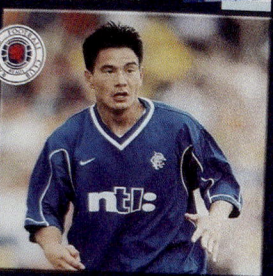

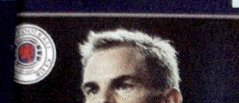

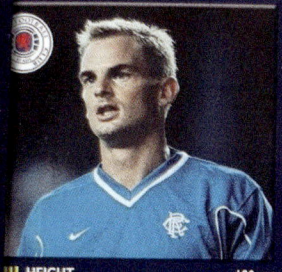

Writers' Association Footballer of the Year and Scottish PFA Players' Player of the Year awards also came his way that year – came another treble; Rangers just managed to snatch the league title from Celtic with both on equal points and a goal difference of +72 to +73. Having stumbled against Dunfermline Athletic and needing a replay to qualify, they went on to lift the Scottish Cup with a 1-0 win over Dundee, and the League Cup (having not stumbled over Dunfermline this time) with a 2-1 win over Celtic.

It was no fault of the new manager Alex McLeish that Rangers were beginning to find their finances strained, which led to an exodus of players, one of whom was Barry Ferguson, who left in August 2003 having scored 18 goals during his time with the club. However, McLeish was held responsible by fans for signing less than sparkling players resulting in seven consecutive losses to Celtic which left them trailing Celtic in second place in the league with 81 points to 98, an unenviable and unwished-for record. In all, there were seven losses in the league competition for 2003-04, a washout season that left the club without trophies again.

McLeish knew that at this level of football he had to deliver and fast, almost was not going to be good enough.

In came Spanish forward Nacho Novo for a mere £0.45m, but never a better silver penny was spent, for the Spaniard became top goalscorer in the 2004-05 season with 25 put away. Barry Ferguson couldn't stay away so he was back, and with two new forwards in the shapes of Dado Pršo and Alex Rae plus defenders Grégory Vignal and Marvin Andrews and several other signings becoming first team regulars, this was a year the manager could breathe a sigh of relief… even though the Scottish Premier League was a race to the finish and won by a whisker, one point, from Celtic. And it was Celtic who gave Rangers the first headache in August 2004 taking all the points in a 1-0 win in the fourth game of the season. That spurred the Light Blues to a 27-game unbeaten league run. It wasn't a season of multiple goal feasts, but a 5-0 win against Aberdeen wasn't a bad afternoon's work, Novo scoring two and defender Fernando Ricksen getting in on the act with a superb low drive from outside the penalty area. Third-placed Hibernian went down in every match against the Gers and Celtic lost two of their subsequent matches as well.

SNAKES AND LADDERS

It wasn't until March 2005 that Rangers truly wobbled, only managing a draw at home against Inverness Caledonian Thistle 1-1. Then they almost completely cut their own legs off with a home loss against Dundee United, 1-0, before practically giving fans a heart attack with a 2-1 defeat to Celtic at Ibrox just twelve days later. There were no more slip-ups, however, and everything then depended on the final match. It was Celtic who blinked first, unexpectedly, at Motherwell, and with the Rangers delivering a 1-0 victory over Hibernian, the helicopter transporting the league trophy had to do an about turn in midair and drop off its cargo to Rangers. All was well at Ibrox.

All the more so because there was already silverware to boast of. The double had been on the cards since March when Rangers had put on a firework show against Motherwell in the League Cup Final. Centre-back Sotirios Kyrgiakos was in place to score 2 goals in the 5-1 dismantling of the Motherwell squad and secure the cup for the Glasgow club.

THE RANGERS TEAM CELEBRATE AFTER THE CIS INSURANCE CUP FINAL MATCH BETWEEN CELTIC AND GLASGOW RANGERS HELD ON MARCH 16, 2003 AT HAMPDEN PARK IN GLASGOW

As Rangers had been turfed out of the Scottish Cup competition by Celtic, 2-1, in January, had the League Cup not fallen to them, McLeish's head might well have been on the block.

It was a rare goal bonanza, but before we leave this season it's worth just touching on that 7-1 semifinal victory over Dundee United in the League Cup competition when Novo and Thompson both put two into the United net as Rangers romped into the final.

It was reasonable to expect that Rangers would do well the following season; it was not to be. In fact, the club blanked out for two seasons and the first one did indeed cost McLeish his job. By February 2006, the decision had been made that McLeish would no longer manage the team.

Defender Julien Rodriguez was the most significant acquisition of the 2005-06 season; not that his presence helped greatly, because Rangers went down to seven defeats in a season that left them on third place at the end. Between the 14th of August 2005 and the 1st of December 2005 they only won four out of fifteen matches. Two successful stretches produced first eight and then twelve games without defeat saving their blushes at the end of the season. Hibernian kicked them out of the Scottish Cup and Celtic did the same in the League Cup. The only brief light was Rangers reaching the last 16 of the Champions League. No Scottish team had got that far since 1993. Villarreal killed the dream, however, going through on away goals.

So ended the most dismal season for many a year.

To be followed by an equally dismal year in which they managed to slide into second place in the league on 72 points, behind Celtic with 84. This time Dunfermline took them out of the Scottish Cup and St. Johnstone did the honours in the League Cup.

There were almost as many managers in the backroom that season as there were losses on the pitch. It was destabilising, but all for the best.

RANGERS PLAYERS CELEBRATE WITH THE SCOTTISH PREMIER LEAGUE TROPHY DURING THE BANK OF SCOTLAND SCOTTISH PREMIER LEAGUE MATCH BETWEEN HIBERNIAN AND RANGERS AT EASTER ROAD STADIUM ON MAY 22, 2005

Paul Le Guen was brought in to replace McLeish, and his disastrous record did nothing to endear him to Rangers fans. Spirits fell amongst the spectators as the Gers set out into the worst start to a season since 1978-79, and the defeat by St. Johnstone in the Scottish League Cup meant that Rangers had been knocked out by a squad from the lower league at home in a cup tournament for the first time in their history. Then Barry Ferguson was removed from the captaincy only for the Le Guen to find himself removed from the managership of the club on the 4th of January 2007. He had the dubious honour of being the club's shortest serving manager at the time.

In came former Rangers' midfielder Ian Durrant doing duty as caretaker manager, soon to be replaced by old faithful Walter Smith on January the 10th, too late to turn the bus around, however. He would lead the club until 2011 and Ally McCoist returned to assist him.

But there would be no more seasons without silver in a Walter Smith season, of that he was certain, and of that he made absolutely sure.

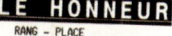

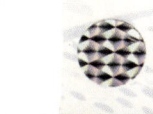

RANGERS MIDFIELDERS BARRY FERGUSON (R) AND BARRY HEMDANI (L) VIES WITH AUXERRE'S MIDFIELDER BENOIT CHEYROU DURING THEIR UEFA CUP FOOTBALL MATCH, AT THE ABBE DESCHAMPS STADIUM IN AUXERRE 23 NOVEMBER 2006

BACK TO THE FRONT

Walter Smith's first full season back at Ibrox, 2007-08, came in the middle of Kris Boyd's five-season run as top goalscorer. He gifted Smith a returning present of 25 goals, and 31 the season after that.

There was new blood, most notably centre-back Carlos Javier Cuéllar Jiménez, who sadly only remained with the club for one season after an injury and who picked up the Scottish Premier League Player of the Year and Scottish Football Writers' Association Player of the Year awards in 65 appearances for Rangers, a record for a single season at Ibrox. Thus armed, Rangers returned to form with a vengeance.

They delivered an exhilarating league season. And it should have been a Premier League-winning season, too, but after a terrific start with five victories, including a 7-2 thrashing handed out to Falkirk, the club experienced two periods when they forgot what the goal looked like; the first of those periods started in September with a loss to Heart of Midlothian 2-4. Three losses in six games meant the race with Celtic was going to be hotter than it should have been even though the Light Blues hacked at their rivals chances by dishing out a 3-0 walloping on the 20th of October 2007.

They then embarked on a glorious nineteen-match run without defeat taking out Celtic, Heart of Midlothian, Dundee and anybody else who dared to challenge them.

After that came the nightmare to end all nightmares; two back-to-back defeats against Celtic in April 2008, 2-1 and 3-2. Which meant that instead of riding high and clear, Rangers were going to have to fight for their lives down to the last league match of the season. And with a UEFA Cup Final and three other competitive matches over the last eight days, the club was going to face a Herculean task. And there was to be no extension

KEVIN THOMSON OF RANGERS VIES WITH LIONEL MESSI OF BARCELONA DURING THE UEFA CHAMPIONS LEAGUE, GROUP E MATCH BETWEEN RANGERS AND BARCELONA AT IBROX STADIUM, OCTOBER 23, 2007

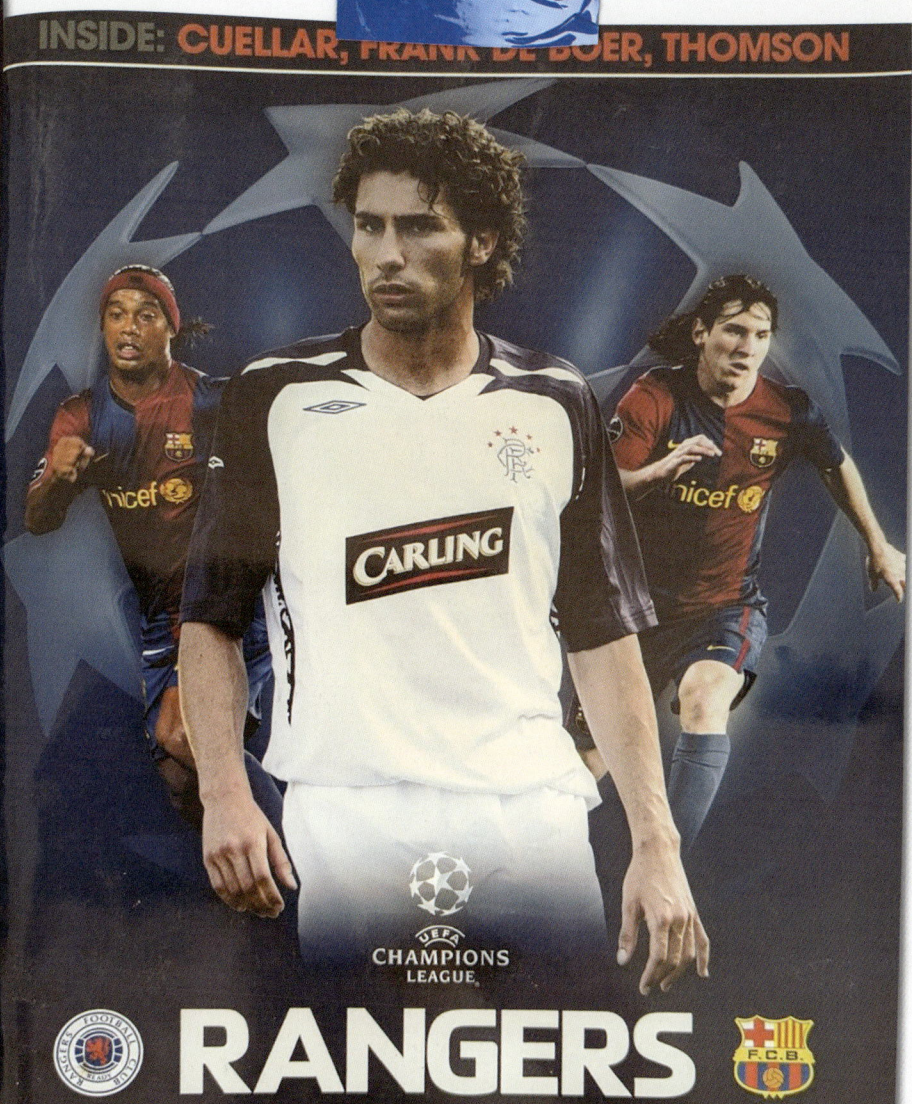

of the season by the SFA to help Rangers; in contrast to their Russian opponents in that cup final, who were given three weeks to prepare free of competition matches.

Nonetheless, the Light Blues fought like tigers, and the results had fans loving their club even more, if that were possible. Walter Smith admitted that he and the club had not really reckoned with getting this far in the UEFA competition and that it was difficult not to allow the magnificent prospect of the cup final taking over everyone's thoughts.

That final league match took place on the 22nd of May 2008 against Aberdeen, a club that was over 30 points behind them in the league. And there should not have been a problem were it not for the fact that on the 14th of May, Rangers had appeared in that UEFA Cup Final, a magnificent achievement by itself.

The team had survived a battering by Fiorentina in the UEFA semi-final by the time they lined up against Russian club Zenit Saint Petersburg, managed by former Rangers manager Dick Advocaat. Smith had opted to keep Kris Boyd, and Novo on the bench and his team was Neil Alexander, Kirk Broadfoot, David Weir, Carlos Cuellar, Sasa Papac, Brahim Hemdani, Steven Whittaker, Barry Ferguson, Kevin Thomson, Steve Davis, Jean-Claude Darcheville.

Rangers were settling in for a smooth defensive game with the lone striker Jean-Claude Darcheville lurking in enemy territory. So although Zenit had the lion's share of the play

Jean-Claude Darcheville (left) and Brahim Hemdani (right) congratulate Rangers scorer Kris Boyd, 09 February 2008

and the first half ended 0-0, there was still everything to play for and Darcheville had proven that he was capable of winning the game when he forced the Russian goalkeeper to smother the Frenchman's shot after an ice-smooth Ranger's move. But Zenit were always dangerous and with two strikes in the second half they eventually left the field 2-0 victors, only the second Russian side to do so. Disappointment, then but no time to stop and mourn.

Next up were Aberdeen in the final league game on which the title depended. Rangers could not summon up the spark required, were unexpectedly hit with two goals and unable to reply. How galling for that result to hand Celtic the league title.

And still no time to mourn, for the Scottish Cup Final against Queen of the South loomed two days later. For a tiring Rangers squad, this tie that should have been a romp home lurked menacingly in view of the recent two lost games and cramped timetable.

Mr. Kris Boyd, however, may have been denied glory in the match against Zenit, but he was about to show that unquenchable spirit that has fed and continues to feed Rangers today.

Rangers began below par in game in which the two sides largely cancelled each other out. However, the best crack at goal, from Rangers, after 25 minutes ignited the flame. And then Boyd struck. And how.

From a free kick outside the penalty area and through the Queen of the South line up Boyd fired an extraordinary swerving ball that left his boot at the speed of light, into the top corner of the net. It then took the ever-dangerous Beasley to find space and rocket in number two just ten minutes later on the 43rd minute. Rangers were back in action.

But it proved too soon to celebrate, because Queen of the South rejuvenated their forces at half-time and struck back rapidly on the 50th and 53rd minutes to pull level. Fans' hearts were in their mouths until the 71st minute. But Kris Boyd was right in front of the goalmouth when a cross came over, and he made it look easy as he slipped the ball off his head and into the net. It was over. Rangers had survived the rigours of a daunting football schedule, delivered wonderful football and been rewarded for their tenacity with the Scottish Cup.

Which was not all they had acquired that season of course, because in March they had dampened down a spirited Dundee United leaving them with a draw in the League Cup Final, 2-2 – who else but the irrepressible Kris Boyd scoring both goals – and conquered them in the penalty shootout, 3-2. So an exhausting season had bought bitter disappointment but great joy as well, in the form of another domestic double.

And that is how it stayed for the following three seasons. Rangers reacquired first place in the league in those three seasons adding the Scottish Cup the first time around, and the League Cup the second and third times around.

There were too many highlights to mention over those years, years when a Kris Boyd hat-trick could be enjoyed;

RANGERS SCRAPBOOK

HUGE CROWDS WATCH NOVO SCORE THE ONLY GOAL IN THE SCOTTISH CUP FINAL AGAINST FALKIRK, 30 MAY 2009

December 2008 for example in a 7-1 flattening of poor Hamilton Academical, or Novo scoring the winning and only goal in the Cup Final against Falkirk in 2009. Kris Boyd with four strikes, this time against Dundee United in the league in another seven-goal romp in December one year later. Miller scoring the winning and only goal in the League Cup Final in March 2010, waiting until the 84th minute to end the tooth-grinding tension – and Rangers had only nine men on the field. Or the cliff-hanger league season of 2010-11, beating Celtic to the top by one point, 93 to 92. Not forgetting the League Cup victory over them as well thanks to Irishman Steven Davis and Croatian forward Nikica Jelavić. Did he have to wait until the 98th minute to do it, though?!

And, yes, there was another match where seven Rangers' goals went in; the boot of Lafferty gave him a hat-trick and Jelavić scored two in a 7-2 day out against Dunfermline in September 2010.

With the quality that Rangers consistently delivered, what could they not achieve? Players of the calibre of James Beattie, Steven Naismith, Kyle Lafferty, Allan McGregor, Saša Papac and Kenny Miller were producing football of top-class standards. They seemed on the brink of cutting the Gordian Knot of European competition soon, and the next treble was certainly just waiting for them to pick up.

All was not what it seemed at Ibrox, though. The excellence on the pitch was not being matched in the backrooms; there, the flames were rising. The club was in financial trouble again, only this time the trouble would not lie down but would explode spectacularly and horrendously in everyone's faces.

BACK TO THE FRONT

SCOTTISH CUP FINAL.
RANGERS V FALKIRK. HAMPDEN - GLASGOW.
ALLY MCCOIST (RIGHT) GETS A KISS
FROM SCORER NACHO NOVO,
30 MAY, 2009

A KNIFE

After eight trophies won in his second spell with Rangers, Walter Smith had called it a day. For the Light Blues' 130th season of football, Ally McCoist stepped into Smith's shoes. He was to be confronted with the financial problems in his attempts to secure new players. "It's going to get worse before it gets better. But one thing is, I want to do everything here. This is my club", he said, adding that he was aware of what was going on and was not scared of the situation the club found itself in.

Little did he realise what was about to happen.

And it had all started so favourably. Twenty games without a loss to get fans dreaming. Four goals put past Celtic and Dunfermline Athletic, three past Dundee and Motherwell. Nikica Jelavić firing on all cylinders closely followed by new signing, forward Omatsone Folarin "Sone" Aluko, who would get his maiden hat-trick during a 4-0 victory over St. Johnstone on the last day of the season. Sadly, he would leave the club in July 2012, caught up in the mighty kerfuffle that was to engulf the club.

Celtic were left far behind in the league... until, gradually, the losses began to mount; seven at season's end, by which time two losses to Celtic had been suffered and the shine came off Rangers' challenge. Aluko, Andrew Little and Kyle Lafferty ran their legs off to make up for the defeats but it was to no avail. Celtic ran away with the championship by twenty points, 93 to 73. By then, the full awfulness of the financial tangle had become known and Rangers had far worse to contend with than the round five exit from the Scottish Cup and the round three exit from the League Cup competition.

Meanwhile, by 2009 Rangers owed some £18 million to Lloyds Banking Group and HMRC had lodged a petition alleging a non-payment of some £9m in PAYE and VAT. On the 14th of February 2012, having

WALTER SMITH AND ALLY MCCOIST ASSISTANT MANAGER CELEBRATE AFTER WINNING THE CLYDESDALE BANK PREMIER LEAGUE AT RUGBY PARK ON MAY 15, 2011

failed in their efforts to avoid it, the club entered into administration. The SPL automatically deducted 10 points from Rangers, which put an end to their hopes of league success, as reports emerged that the club might be in debt to the tune of 134 million pounds.

A consortium under British businessman Charles Green bought the club for £2 from Craig Whyte, who had sent ripples of fear through the boardroom that he would not be able to invest in the club when he bought it in 2011. As the smog cleared, the club then passed

IN THE HEART

into the hand of another consortium, Sevco Scotland Ltd., for which £5.5m changed hands. Thus from the ashes of the old was born The Rangers Football Club Ltd.

In September 2014 as the fallout continued, Whyte was banned from being a company director for 15 years and then arrested for alleged fraud related to Rangers before being declared bankrupt in October 2015. Rangers FC, then still owing £21 million of £55 million worth of debt, would be formally liquidated on the 8th of January 2015.

Rangers players and fans did not deserve to be witnesses to, or have their loyalty rewarded by, these blackest of days in Rangers' long history, foisted upon them by events beyond their control.

The rumours crashing around the stands at Ibrox affected the players, of course, and most top players refused to be transferred to the new company. A whole raft of players left the club; captain David Weir on the 17th of January, Nikica Jelavić on the 31st of January, James Beattie on the 31st of August, and several others. Unable to secure a place in the Scottish Premier League – on the 4th of July, ten of the other eleven Premiership clubs had voted against them staying in the Premier League – Rangers had to accept entering the Scottish Football League instead. Having been awarded associate membership, the club was not even allowed to join the First Division, but was dumped into the Third Division. It was a bitter humiliation.

November 2012 saw Walter Smith return as a non-executive director. The club was also subjected to a twelve-month transfer ban starting on the 1st of September, bringing with it the inability to register any players over eighteen years of age. Ally McCoist, nonetheless, held true to the club he loved, determined to help bring it back to where it rightfully belonged.

WALTER SMITH, MANAGER OF RANGERS HOLDS THE SCOTTISH PREMIER LEAGUE TROPHY AFTER WINNING THE CLYDESDALE BANK PREMIER LEAGUE AT RUGBY PARK ON MAY 15, 2011

HERCULES

In autumn 2012, McCoist was forced to field a team that was very unlike the one he had managed in the summer. Left back Lee Wallace also stayed loyal, becoming captain in 2015; Lee McCulloch was another old faithful (he eventually totted up 26 goals in the season) as was midfielder Kyle Hutton. And Andy Little was back and would prove to be a pivotal player in the arduous climb back to the top.

A climb that started in a very odd manner in August 2012 with only three wins in seven games. Odd, because each win was a whopper; 5-1 against East Stirlingshire, 5-1 against Elgin City and 4-1 against Montrose. The loss was a 1-0 against Stirling Albion, and other games were 2-2, 1-1 and 0-0 draws. Best not to ask. No Scottish Cup, League Cup or Scottish Challenge Cup. Long story short, Rangers won the division with 83 points and were promoted. League Division One... sigh.

So the good thing to report about the 2013-14 season was the league challenge. A glance at the table, even in Division One, is a joy to behold. Not one single defeat. And a good sprinkling of the four and five-goal lashings that Rangers can deal out when they're in the mood. Not to mention the 8-0 wipeout of Stenhousemuir in which new arrival Jonathan Daly thumped in four. Promotion to the Championship followed the league title, won with 102 points, Dunfermline Athletic in second place on 63. No cups, but the main thing was the promotion; so, Championship... sigh.

What to say about the first Championship season? Probably as little as possible. Nicky Law was top goalscorer with a miserly 13.

ALLY MCCOIST DURING THE RAMSDENS CUP QUARTER FINAL. RANGERS V QOTS. IBROX - GLASGOW. RANGERS MANAGER

MCCOIST

The revolving door was swinging again as Ally McCoist departed on the 21st of December, his place taken temporarily by Kenny McDowell until March when he resigned and was replaced by Stuart McCall, who would only remain until the 15th of June 2015, not a great situation for players, who need at least a reasonable amount of stability in which to prepare and play. So under the circumstances, it was a miracle that the lads managed to get into two semi-finals; the League Cup and the Challenge Cup.

After 33 goals, Andrew Little was on the move and left the club. Kris Boyd had returned, although only for the one season, to hit ten goals. An indication of the state of mind the team was in. Probably the highlight of the Championship season was the 6-1 jaunt against Raith Rovers, which was squeezed in amongst a welter of losses and draws, a game in which fans could enjoy Mr. Daly scoring two and Mr. Boyd also hitting the back of the net.

Most disappointing of all, of course, the play-off for the Premiership. Having reached the final, albeit not without a struggle, Motherwell dashed any faint hopes left by serving up 3-1 and 3-0 defeats. The rise through the ranks had been stopped. But Rangers would not be kept out of top-flight Premiership football for long.

June 2015. It was now Mark Warburton's chance to have a go at getting Rangers to produce the sparkle; manager number fourteen. Not an easy task with the distracting background noise continuing, a £7.5 million club loss and Charles Green and Craig Whyte arrested in September. Then, Arnold Peralta, a player who had only just left the club in January and returned to Honduras was shot eighteen times in his hometown, La Ceiba, and murdered.

New arrivals lined up: Marty Waghorn, top goalscorer with 28 goals, defender James Tavernier, midfielder Andy Halliday, midfielder Jason Holt and American midfielder Gedion Zelalem amongst others, to face St. Mirren. With a great deal of trepidation, fans trooped into Ibrox.

And the goal feasts began again!

Lee Wallace was so eager to get going, he hit his first goal after 4 minutes and the second after 26 with forward Dean Shiels finishing the 3-1 victory. In the next four matches,

Rangers struck home 5 times in three of them and banged in four against Greenock Morton in an eleven-game undefeated march upwards to start the season. Thankfully the Gers produced another eleven-game undefeated run later in the season, because they lurched into the buffers in March 2016 and won just two of the last eight games. Fortunately for them they were far enough ahead of Falkirk to take the title with 81 points to Falkirk and Hibernian's 70 apiece and secured the title with their last victory, against Dumbarton, in April.

After five years of turmoil, Warburton and the Gers had finally clambered back into the Premiership.

A Hibernian injury time winner snatched the Scottish Cup away from them, 2-3, but there was more silverware in the Challenge Cup, where a run of victories had led them to the final against Peterhead.

No mistakes this time. Tavernier, Halliday and Miller, with help from an own goal saw Rangers take the spoils.

Rangers never looked like losing, pressuring from the start, taking the game to Peterhead and forcing the error that led to the first own goal. Tavernier's strike was an absolute beauty as the ball was gently chipped to his foot by Miller before he volleyed in a scorcher from just outside the box. A goalmouth scare was blocked on the line and a misfired shot had fans' hearts in their mouths, but Rangers continued to surge forward time and time again jinking and swerving past the opposition. They produced riveting moves in front of the Peterhead goal which should have made it three but had to wait until the 85th minute for a penalty for Halliday to bring another goal. Not enough, more razor-sharp penetration brought Miller into space, and when the ball came unexpectedly to his feet, in it went.

KENNY MILLER OF RANGERS HOLDS THE TROPHY DURING THE PETROFAC TRAINING CUP FINAL BETWEEN RANGERS AND PETERHEAD AT HAMPDEN PARK ON APRIL 10, 2016

GOODBYE CHAMPIONSHIP

Generally, the new arrivals were less prominent than the veteran Rangers players, though defender Clint Hill proved his worth and forward Joe Garner was the third-best goalscorer with ten to his credit.

Any hopes that were harboured of a swift ascent to the top of the Premiership were stymied early on, however, with only two victories from six games and a black eye from Celtic, 5-1. Then a bad run of only three wins in twelve games put paid to the season completely. With 67 points, the Gers trailed in third place behind champions Celtic on 106. Neither did the Scottish or League Cup yield more than a semi-final, and then Celtic bounced Rangers out of both those competitions as well. There was clearly a lot of work to be done.

As had happened so often to the Rangers players, instability was not caused by them but by the shenanigans in the back rooms. Manager Mark Warburton put on his hat and left in February of 2017 following criticism of his failure to recruit new, permanent, playing talent. Assistant manager David Weir went with him so there was no one to maintain continuity. Graeme Murty was transferred from his post as head coach of the development squad to become caretaker manager of the first eleven. In March, he was replaced by Portuguese coach Pedro Miguel Faria Caixinha. A breathing space, finally, though the season was beyond repair.

Which, to everyone's frustration and anger, is how it remained for the following three seasons.

At least a new hero on the field had arrived to bring cheer; Colombian striker Alfredo José Morelos Aviléz, who was to make the top goalscorer spot his own

for the three successive seasons, and started his run sharing the honour with Josh Windass on 18 apiece. Which helped to close the gap on Celtic at the final whistle of the season but still left the team in 3rd place, twelve points adrift. The performance cleft between Rangers and Celtic remained open, as the 4-0 semi-final defeat in the Scottish Cup semi-final proved unequivocally in April 2018. Rangers struggled to maintain their form and suffered ten losses in the league, one of which had been another painful 5-0 defeat to Celtic, with three sets of back-to-back losses scarring their league performance record.

The best result came late, in April 2018 in the match against Dundee, when Rangers hauled in a 4-0 victory with goals from Miller, Morelos, Murphy and Candeias. Candeias' terrific outing culminated with him hammering the ball home after a pass from fellow new boy that season, midfielder Graham Dorrans. At least the effort brought the team to second in the table. Briefly. A moment of hope but no new trophies after the final game of the season; a 5-5 goal spectacular against Hibernian to send fans home with at least some hopeful excitement.

BETFRED CUP. RANGERS V DUNFERLINE.
IBROX - GLASGOW. RANGERS' ALFREDO
MORELOS CELEBRATES HIS GOAL.
09 AUGUST, 2017

Morelos' improved scoring average in the season that followed, showed that improvement had taken place all round in the team. His impressive tally of 30 came in tandem with a second place in the league. Tantalisingly close to glory now.

A lack of expected good results meant that a fresh face had taken on the task of coaching the team; England and Liverpool legend Steven Gerrard.

Josh Windass and Kenny Miller had moved on but captain James Tavernier was firing on all cylinders picking up 17 goals despite his role as defender. Another impressive new signing was Canadian international midfielder Scott Airfield, who would secure his permanent position for the following seasons with his performance.

Gerrard got off to a racing start, unbeaten in the first 12 games. At last, Rangers had got the measure of Celtic and downed them twice, sadly, however, falling to Aberdeen in

HELLO NEW WORLD

RANGERS SCRAPBOOK

STEVEN GERRARD IS UNVEILED AS THE NEW MANAGER OF RANGERS FOOTBALL CLUB AT IBROX STADIUM ON MAY 4, 2018

the Scottish and League Cup challenges. There had still been too many losses in the league, six, to get to the top spot but the gap was gradually closing; 78 to Celtic's 87. Second place. And the lads were producing some sizzling football again and bringing in those multi-goal victories for which they were famous; 5-2 against St Johnstone, 7-2 against Motherwell, 5-0 against Hamilton Academical. Plus 4-0 wins against St Mirren and Dundee. But the Gers couldn't crack Kilmarnock, third-placed at season's end, drawing twice and then losing to them 2-1 twice.

Against the run of play in the last game of the season when Rangers had played some terrific fast and dangerous football, and hit the bar, Kilmarnock scored when Burke was allowed easy access. From then on, an exciting match produced moments of delight and tension and it took until the 66th minute for Morelos' magic to even the scores after a breathtaking move by Rangers that enabled Morelos to fire the ball into the net from close range.

GOODBYE CHAMPIONSHIP, HELLO NEW WORLD

Alas, all was in vain, for a Kilmarnock penalty brought the curtain crashing down on another season.

So Rangers went into their 140th season of competitive football and the season when a little known virus worked its way through the entire world and panic set in; 2019-20.

Rangers began again in fine style, absolutely destroying Hibernian 6-1 in the second match, striker Jermain Defoe claiming a hat-trick. Aberdeen, Hamilton and Hearts watched five goals hurtle past them as Rangers set off to enjoy twenty games with just one loss – to Celtic. Was this an omen. Well, December brought Rangers to Celtic Park, where they battled to a 2-1 victory, their first win there since October 2010. The League Cup final was reached but lost in another Old Firm clash.

The New Year brought a collapse in form; Heart of Midlothian won the Scottish Cup quarter-final tie by a single goal, and there were just four league wins in nine games. The league title had to be conceded to Celtic yet again, an event that was becoming boringly monotonous and needed a new narrative.

Steven Gerrard went into the summer and somehow came back with the magic formula. The defending wall at the back was rock solid with left-back Borna Barišić, Joe Aribo was prowling in midfield and Kemar Roofe and Cedric Itten had come to join Defoe and Morelos up front. And Rangers' now iconic goalkeeper Alan McGregor, back with the team since 2018, was holding his lonely, heroic vigil again. The Rangers sparkle of old was well and truly back.

The Light Blues almost completed a clean sweep, but didn't lose a single match in the league, whilst producing goal feasts,

19 from James Tavernier, for the fans to talk about for years to come. In 32 wins and six draws, they conceded just 13 goals, a new British record. Both Gerrard and Tavernier would garner a host of awards that season. The team ran away with the Premiership title in spectacular style firing up to the top to gain a club record of 102 points, far above a Celtic team reduced to trailing them with just 77.

Impossible to filter out all the highlights, the season was awash with them. Forget the 8-0 walkabout over poor Hamilton Academical, Roofe, Aribo and Tavernier netting two apiece. Glorious.

Here's one, though. It had to be a tough game, for although Hibernian and Aberdeen were eagerly on the hunt that season, they were no match for a resurgent Rangers. No, it has to be Celtic and that match on the 2nd of May 2021. Played in front of a practically empty stadium, sadly.

The triumvirate of Roofe, Morelos and Defoe were on fire that day, a day to have been at Ibrox.

26 minutes into the first half with the ball moving from end to end and heart-stopping chances coming and vanishing. Borna Barišić was gaining a lot of possession out on the left wing and Kent was working hard on the right wing. One of several fabulous saves by keeper McGregor sent the ball against the bar but Rangers kept up the pressure, and sure enough, Roofe managed to be in the path of a rising ball from Ryan Kent and with a skilled twist of his body redirected the ball into the net.

A momentary lapse in attention allowed Celtic to head an equaliser and maintain the tension, and then a superb bit of leg work by Morelos inside the box just three minutes later, which he topped by firing home a left foot rising drive, sent the temperature up again.

Then came an extraordinary goal by Roofe again, on the 57th minute. Having jinked and passed the ball out to the wing, he hurtled forward past the defence, unmarked, in a genius moment of premonition as the lofted ball sailed over the knot of defenders, and without missing a beat Roofe headed the ball into the net. A glorious Rangers moment.

Celtic remained dangerous, but two minutes into injury time Defoe was given the ball three-quarters of the way down the field, from where he jinked and twisted his way into the Celtic box before a low left-foot drive saw number four underline Rangers' domination of the match and the season.

The win meant that in all competitions, Rangers had won all three home games against Celtic and not lost any of the Old Firm fixtures, becoming the first Light Blues squad to achieve that since the 1999-00 season.

Roofe finished the season with another two goals in the 4-0 win over Aberdeen and Rangers had ended the drought. The Premiership title was theirs after years in the desert and a long struggle back to the top to regain the place they so deserved.

GOODBYE CHAMPIONSHIP, HELLO NEW WORLD

JAMES TAVERNIER OF RANGERS JUMPS TO HEADS THE BALL DURING THE LADBROKES SCOTTISH PREMIERSHIP MATCH BETWEEN RANGERS AND CELTIC AT IBROX STADIUM ON DECEMBER 31, 2016

KEMAR ROOFE SCORES TO MAKE IT 1-0 RANGERS DURING A SCOTTISH PREMIERSHIP MATCH BETWEEN RANGERS AND CELTIC AT IBROX PARK, ON MAY 02, 2021

FORWARD TO THE FUTURE

JOHN LUNDSTRAM (C) CELEBRATES AFTER SCORING THEIR THIRD GOAL DURING THE UEFA EUROPA LEAGUE SEMI-FINAL, SECOND LEG FOOTBALL MATCH BETWEEN RANGERS AND RB LEIPZIG AT THE IBROX, ON MAY 5, 2022

Jermain Defoe bid farewell after sterling work at the club as Gerrard and his team entered the fray for 2021-22.

Rangers, it seemed, were not to be granted peace when they most needed it, for in November Gerrard pulled the plug and Giovanni van Bronckhorst stepped in to breach the gap. It was not an easy task, but he hit the ground running and enabled Rangers to keep up the fight bringing the club to within a whisker of double cup glory.

At the beginning of the season, the second game was bit of a downer, a loss 1-0 to Dundee United, but the recovery saw 21 games without defeat. Rangers were fighting hard. Although the League Cup challenge petered out in the semi-final, Roofe and Airfield ensured that Celtic were booted out of the Scottish Cup and a Rangers' encounter in the final set up against Hearts on the 21st of May, three days after the Europa Cup final. That was going to be a tough call whatever happened in Spain.

And to prove that Rangers were cementing their claim to the very top ranks of football, there was more excitement in the UEFA Europa League, where the Gers had fought their way through to the semi-final against German team RB Leipzig. If anyone had known what was going to happen then, they would not have been able to sleep for a month.

In the league as May 2022 came around, the team found itself six points behind Celtic with four games to play, the first of which was a clash at Celtic Park. It was a vital match to keep the title challenge alive. On the 28th of April came the all-important clash with Leipzig in the Europa League semi-final. It did not go as planned and Rangers fans were left with that sinking feeling as they trooped home after a 1-0 defeat. Sadly, before the second leg took place there was another death to mourn. Rangers' kit man of long standing, Jimmy Bell, died unexpectedly aged 69.

The Germans celebrated too quickly, however, for Rangers were now surging and playing their hearts out, and in the 79th minute came a move that will be displayed in gold in the Ranger's history books. Tavernier sent over a high free kick that found Ryan Kent's magic feet. He shook off the challenge to send over a cross high in front of the goal and over the keeper's head. The ball dropped to midfielder John Lundstram, who, with all the power of Ibrox behind him fired in a low hard shot. It was Rangers, after a superb fightback, who were going to the Europa League final in Seville.

The Premiership challenge could not overcome the three losses, despite the Gers holding Celtic to a 1-1 draw at Celtic Park, and the club finished second once again, although the three-point difference between Rangers and Celtic showed just how close the Gers had come to the league winners. Nonetheless, the 3-1 defeat of Hearts away from home led to hope that the Scottish Cup final against the same opponents was going to produce a similar result.

Wednesday May 18th 2022 came to an end with a lost Europa League final in Seville against German club Eintracht Frankfurt. And yet, it had been Rangers who had taken the lead. Easily the equals of the German team, it was the penalty shoot-out that decided the fate of the Gers, and fate was not on their side. Perhaps not the best game Rangers have ever played, but once they got into their stride they could have pulled it off. But 1-1 led to the shoot-out and it was not to be with Eintracht taking the honours 5-4.

Now, however, Rangers had to try and find reserves of energy to produce a cup-winning performance in the Scottish Cup final against Hearts on the 21st of May just

On the 5th of May, Ibrox was bursting as Rangers hosted the confident German side for the second leg. Rangers, without Alfredo Morelos and Kemar Roofe, had an uphill struggle, but they knew what they had to do and they were on fire from the start. It took just 25 minutes for the flames to start rising when Glen Kamara fought like a lion to get the ball through to Ryan Kent, who whipped off down the field to hammer the ball across the Leipzig goal for Tavernier, hovering at the far post, to hurtle in and ram it into the net thus setting the aggregate scores at 1-1. And then a gorgeous, light, Rangers' move that went through the German defence and was delicately and superbly finished by Kamara to put Rangers ahead. Ibrox was delirious.

Rangers were dangerous, threatening with every move, yet in the 69th minute it was Leipzig who pulled one back in a rare lapse of attention in the Rangers' squad.

three days later. It was a Herculean task to ask of any team.

Rangers, however, are not just any team. They were absolutely determined to overcome the intense emotions and physical tiredness after the Europa League final and end the season on a high note.

With five changes to the team that fought in Seville, no McGregor, no Kamara, no Barisic, this final clash, made sweeter by the semi-final defeat of Celtic, 2-1, got off to a nervous if exciting start. It took Rangers twenty minutes to get into their stride, without testing Hearts goalie Gordon very severely, however.

As the second half progressed, both teams were finding it difficult to produce the sharp finishing required to decide the match though as the clock ticked, Rangers were gaining the upper hand and more, though still abortive, chances came their way. As full time approached the pressure on Hearts became ever more intense.

Nonetheless, the game went into extra time. Now Rangers were on full transmission and after a Tavernier corner, Jack Ryan found himself in acres of space outside the Hearts's area as the ball dropped towards him and he let loose all of Rangers' frustration with a dynamite 20-yard shot that struck the roof of the net. At last, Rangers had the lead they deserved. And they kept pressing forward with new waves that reaped their reward shortly after.

It was a glorious Rangers' move. Rangers broke forward from their own half with Ryan Kent coming swiftly forwards rolling the ball as Wright raced into position on the right. Kent pushed his pass to him and Wright, like Ryan before him, unleashed a blistering shot, this one firing low across Gordon and into the net.

The Scottish Cup was firmly in Rangers' hold, and as the final whistle sounded, Rangers had secured their 117th trophy, their first Scottish Cup since 2009, and captain Tavernier could proudly mount the steps and hold the cup on high. How fitting that James Tavernier would end the season as top goalscorer, alongside Alfredo Morelos, for his second season in a row; what a testimony to his importance to the team and what a fabulous ending to a wonderful season for Rangers.

RANGERS CAPTAIN JAMES TAVERNIER LIFTS THE SCOTTISH CUP TROPHY DURING THE SCOTTISH CUP FINAL MATCH BETWEEN RANGERS AND HEARTS AT HAMPDEN PARK, ON MAY 21, 2022

FORWARD TO THE FUTURE

Rangers FC has had a uniquely extraodinary past and is destined for a uniquely extraordinary future. It is the first club in the world to claim more than fifty national league titles, at present the number stands at 55. The club is also the most honoured in the world, winning 116 trophies in total, 55 titles in Scottish leagues, 34 Scottish Cups, 27 League Cups.

Rangers as a club and as a team has fought back against bitter adversity and refused to be kept down, risen to stride proudly through the top ranks of the football world. There have been more than enough tragedies, disappointments and triumphs to make any fan tremble in despair and excitement, but the absolute dedication to the Light Blues that every player, manager and club member has shown, prove that Rangers is no ordinary club; Rangers is a way of life, a life force and a force to reckoned with wherever the team plays. The players will ensure that name of Rangers will always be spoken of in tandem with thrilling football, played by some of the world's most talented players, who will continue to make the club one of the greatest in the world.

THE PLAYERS

IT IS IMPOSSIBLE TO EVEN SCRATCH THE SURFACE WITH A LIST THAT CANNOT HOPE TO ENCOMPASS ALL OF THE MANY, MANY TRULY GREAT PLAYERS THAT HAVE GRACED THE BLUE SHIRTS, BUT LET'S JUST TAKE A LUCKY DIP AND PULL OUT A FEW THAT MUST SURELY BE INCLUDED IN ANY POST-MATCH CONVERSATION ABOUT RANGERS' PAST AND ITS PRESENT.

BRIAN LAUDRUP

Brian Laudrup was Born in Vienna, Austria on the 22nd of February 1969. At the time, his father, Danish international football player Michael, was playing for Wiener SC.

Young Brian started his professional footballing career with Brøndby in Denmark, and as his reputation blossomed he eventually made his way through legendary German team Bayern Munich and then Italian club Florentina, to Scotland and Rangers.

Laudrup was considered to be not only one of the major talents of his generation at Rangers and the Danish national team but in the world, and the 1.86 metres (6ft 1in) tall forward was equally as effective in midfield or on the wings.

He joined Rangers in 1994, and will forever be remembered for the 1996 Scottish Cup Final against Hearts, scoring two goals and setting up three others. Unfortunately, he was often plagued by injuries, which eventually brought about the end of his career just two years after his departure from Rangers in 1998. Laudrup made 116 appearances with the team and scored 33 goals.

Laudrup was a genuinely unselfish player and an excellent reader of the game, a man who could accelerate with the ball, add speed and who displayed technical expertise and ball control. Always on the lookout to create openings for his teammates, his elegance of movement belied the power of his striking capacity. His only weakness lay, perhaps, in his ability to perform with a rigid consistency, but his footballing contemporaries heaped praise upon his sturdy frame.

Laudrup found a career after football as a football commentator and a youth football coach. He and his wife Mette have a son, Nicolai, and a daughter, Rasmine.

BRIAN LAUDRUP AWARDS:

- Danish Player of the Year 1989, 1992, 1995, 1997
- Kicker Bundesliga Team of the Season 1989-90
- Kicker Bundesliga Best Forward 1990-91
- UEFA Euro 1992 Team of the Tournament
- Best Player FIFA Confederations Cup 1995
- SFWA Footballer of the Year 1994-95
- 1998 FIFA World Cup All-Star Team
- FIFA 100
- Denmark Hall of Fame
- Scottish Football Hall of Fame
- Brondby Wall of Honour
- Glasgow Rangers Hall of Fame

JOHN GREIG

John Greig MBE was born on the 11th of September 1942 in Edinburgh, Scotland. The man who spent his entire career with Rangers, joining the first team in 1961, made 755 appearances for the club and returned to manage them between 1978 and 1983. He was also the longest-serving captain for the Rangers team, first taking over the role in 1965 and retaining his position until he retired in 1978. Despite fierce competition for the title – as one Gersnet commentator mentioned it was an accolade that might have fallen to many other contenders such as Mr. Struth, The Founding Fathers, RC Hamilton, Valance, George Young, Bob McPhail or Alan Morton – supporters once voted for Greig as "The Greatest Ever Ranger". A centre back, he was a Scottish National team player on 44 occasions, and a man who can score 120 goals does, indeed, have a record that is truly enviable. Also, it was during his reign as captain that Rangers claimed their only European title to date, the European Cup Winners Cup in 1972.

Having left Rangers, John worked for BBC television and radio Scotland as a pundit and then became part of Rangers public-relations team. Later he became involved in youth development. From 2003 he was on the board of directors for the club, resigning in 2011, finally becoming honorary life president in 2015.

JOHN GREIG AWARDS:
- SFWA Footballer of the Year 1965-66, 1975-76
- Scottish Football Hall of Fame
- Scottish Sports Hall of Fame

MANAGERIAL AWARDS:
- Scottish Cup 1978-79, 1980-81
- Scottish League Cup 1978-79, 1981-82

John Greig is no ordinary skipper
MONEY COULD NOT BUY HIM SAYS WADDELL

JIM BAXTER

Jim Baxter was born on the 29th of September 1939 in Hill of Beath, Fife, Scotland. Jim started his working life as an apprentice to a cabinet maker before spending a period of time down the coal mines. Having been urged by his former headmaster to join the local football team, Jim played for Crossgates Primrose in Fife, before moving onto Raith Rovers with whom he made 62 appearances between 1957 and 1960. But it was when he joined Rangers in 1960 that his career flourished. Now considered one of Scotland's greatest players, "Slim Jim" was a vital pivot at left-half in the team that triumphed in the first years of the 1960s. Even luminary Sir Alex Ferguson, former Manchester United manager, praised Jim Baxter as "arguably the best player to play in Scottish football".

Unfortunately, after a four-month recuperation period following a fractured leg sustained in a match against Rapid Vienna in December 1964, his heavy drinking affected his fitness and he left the club in 1965 after 136 appearances. Baxter's drinking problem meant that he needed two liver transplants within the space of four days after he had become the licensee of a pub upon retirement. And if he wasn't spending money on alcohol he was betting vast amounts on the horses.

His footballing talent brought him 34 Scottish caps and three international goals, four Scottish League Cups, three Scottish Cups and three Scottish League titles.

A notorious joker on the field, he was even more notorious for the calm efficiency of his game, credited with artistry and a unique style that was his own. The fans' were absolutely joyful at his ability to completely wrong-foot his opponents with a deceitful twist of his hips.

Jim had two sons, Alan and Stephen with his wife Jean Ferguson who he married in 1965. The two later divorced and Baxter then found a new partner, Norma Morton, and the two remained together until Jim's death in 2001 from pancreatic cancer.

JIM BAXTER AWARDS:
- Scottish Football Hall of Fame
- Scottish Sports Hall of Fame

ANDY GORAM

Andrew Lewis Goram was born on the 13th of April 1964 in Bury, England, and died on the 2nd of July 2022.

Andy's father Lewis had been a professional footballer in the 1940s and 50s, and Andy always felt himself to be Scottish despite his English place of birth.

His professional career began with West Bromwich Albion, and he moved via Hibernian onto Rangers, joining the club in 1991.

In his years at Rangers, he became known as "the Goalie", and he became a permanent fixture at Ibrox until he left the club in 1998 after 184 appearances.

Andy also became goalkeeper for the Scottish national side for whom he would eventually appear 43 times, vying for the position with Jim Leighton.

Andy's 5ft 11in frame displayed bullet-fast reflexes, and he would dominate opposition players in 'one-on-one' situations, rarely allowing himself to emerge from the confrontation having drawn the short straw.

Andy's resilience was in evidence in 1993 when he needed surgery to repair damage to his knee. His fitness levels took a nose dive and Walter Smith decided that his playing days at Rangers were over. Andy had other ideas. He recovered and was soon back where he belonged wearing the Rangers jersey.

Once he had retired from playing, Andy turned his capable hands to coaching, besides indulging in his other great passion in life, cricket, in which game his talent had been on display for the Scottish National team.

Goram is certainly at the top of the list of the greatest-ever Rangers goalkeepers alongside Alan McGregor, Chris Woods and Stefan Klos, and many Rangers fans, with support from Ally McCoist, consider him to be the cream of the crop.

ANDY GORAM AWARDS:
- SFWA Footballer of the Year 1992–93
- SPFA Players' Player of the Year 1992–93
- Scottish Football Hall of Fame 2010

ALLY McCOIST

Alistair Murdoch McCoist, MBE, was born on the 24th of September 1962 in Bellshill, Scotland and was educated at Maxwellton Primary School and Hunter High School. His first job upon leaving school was as a clerk in the Overseas Development Agency, where flexible working hours allowed him to pursue his dream of a football career.

St. Johnstone was the first professional contract to come McCoist's way and he then moved on to Sunderland before joining Rangers in 1983, where he was to stay until 1998. The 5ft 10in striker also appeared for the Scottish National Team on 61 occasions.

McCoist and Mark Hateley formed a formidable duo and McCoist struck home 355 goals, becoming the club's record goalscorer, and claiming club records for the number of goals scored in the league, 251, and in the Scottish League Cup, 54. In all, he appeared for the club 581 times in his fifteen years.

His razor-edged striking abilities were legendary as his award of the European Golden Shoe twice, 1992 and 1993, proved.

When he retired from football after a spell at Kilmarnock, he took up television presenting and pundit work before returning to Rangers in 2011, where he took over the management of the team from Walter Smith. Despite the burden of severe financial difficulties, McCoist managed to help the team through two successive promotions before leaving in 2014.

In the course of his long career, Ally McCoist has claimed ten Scottish Premier Division titles and nine Scottish Cups.

McCoist met his first wife Allison in 1981 and the pair married in 1990 and they are parents to 3 children, Alexander, Argyll, and Mitchell.

After divorcing from Allison in 2004 he married Vivian, and they have two sons, Arron and Harris.

ALLY McCOIST AWARDS:

- European Golden Shoe 1991–92, 1992–93
- European Cup Top Scorer 1987–88
- SFWA Footballer of the Year 1991–92
- SPFA Players Player of the Year 1991–92
- Awarded the MBE, 10th of June 1994 (for services to football)
- Scottish Premier League Manager of the Month, September 2011
- Scottish League Third Division Manager of the Month, December 2012
- Scottish League One Manager of the Month, September 2013, January 2014
- Scotland National Football Team Roll of Honour 1996

BARRY FERGUSON

Barry Ferguson was born on the 2nd of February 1978 in Hamilton, Scotland. Barry's older brother had played for Rangers in the 1980s, and Barry began his football career playing for Hamilton team Mill United at the age of eight.

Whilst attending Brannock High School, Ferguson began training with Rangers in 1991, and when he finished his education in 1994 he signed with the club professionally.

His first team debut came in 1996 as manager Walter Smith began to acclimatise him to playing with the seasoned professionals.

By 1998 he had become one of the first eleven regulars and an indispensable member of the midfield lineup going on to captain the team at the age of just 22. His performances drew praise from fans, critics and teammates.

When he left the club in 2003 he had made 151 appearances scoring 24 goals. After a short spell of Blackburn Rovers, he was back in the Rangers shirt in 2005, this time for a four-year spell and 137 appearances.

Known for dominating the midfield, his vast work appetite and dictating the pace and flow of a game, Ferguson also captained the team but suffered from injury, which took the shine off his talents somewhat. Nonetheless, up until his second departure from Rangers, he played for the Scottish National team on 45 occasions.

When he retired from playing, he took up management, initially at Blackpool as caretaker before moving onto Clyde and several other clubs.

Barry Ferguson has three children, Connor, Kyle and Kara with his wife Margaret.

BARRY FERGUSON AWARDS:

- PFA Scotland Young Player of the Year, 1998-99
- SFWA Footballer of the Year, 1999-2000, 2002-03
- SPFA Players Player of the Year, 2002-03
- SPL Player of the Month, November 2000, December 2000, February 2002, January 2003
- MBE, 17th of June 2006

MANAGER AWARDS:

- Lowland league, 2019-20, 2020-21

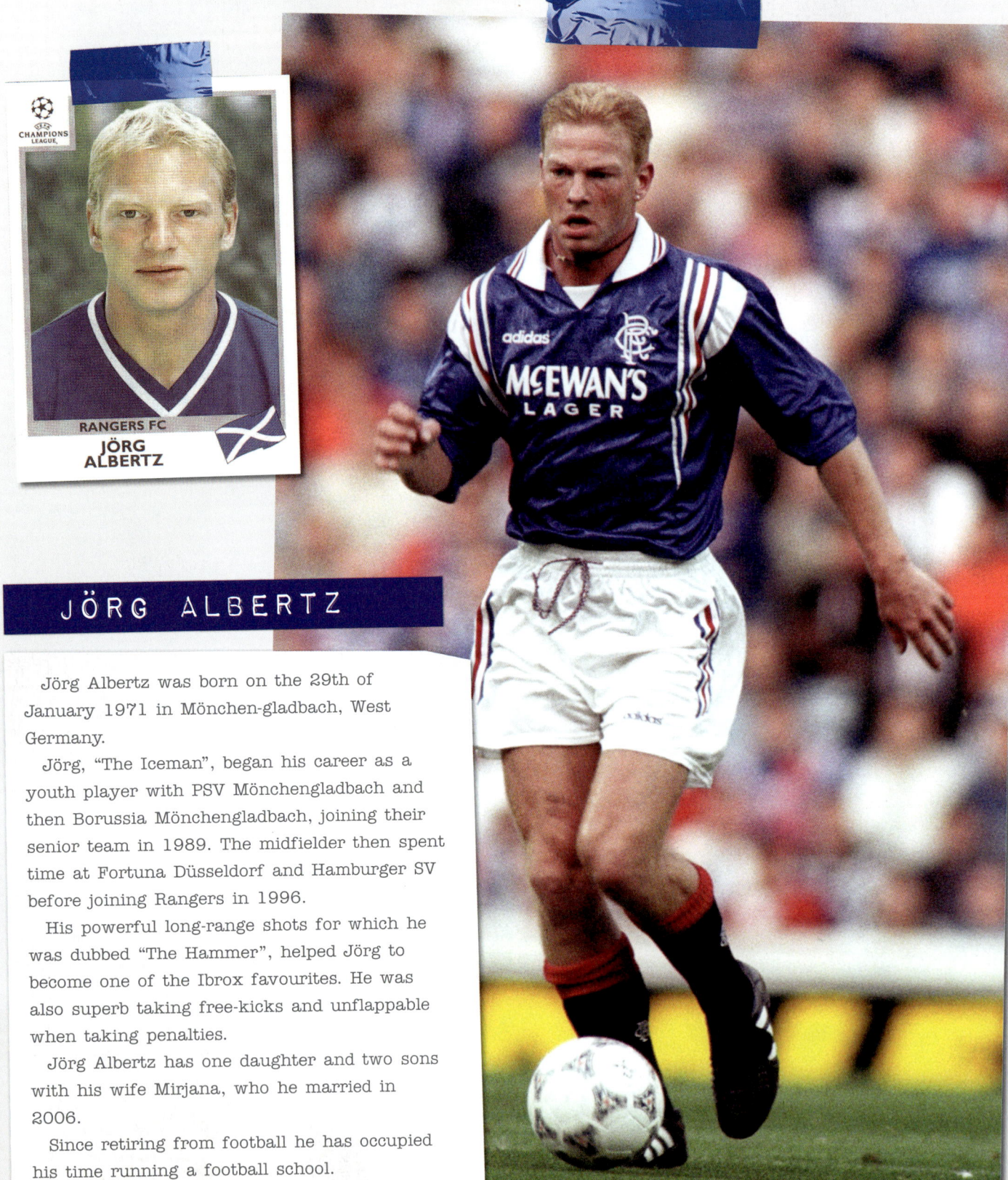

JÖRG ALBERTZ

Jörg Albertz was born on the 29th of January 1971 in Mönchen-gladbach, West Germany.

Jörg, "The Iceman", began his career as a youth player with PSV Mönchengladbach and then Borussia Mönchengladbach, joining their senior team in 1989. The midfielder then spent time at Fortuna Düsseldorf and Hamburger SV before joining Rangers in 1996.

His powerful long-range shots for which he was dubbed "The Hammer", helped Jörg to become one of the Ibrox favourites. He was also superb taking free-kicks and unflappable when taking penalties.

Jörg Albertz has one daughter and two sons with his wife Mirjana, who he married in 2006.

Since retiring from football he has occupied his time running a football school.

DAVIE COOPER

Davie Cooper was born on the 25th of February 1956 in Hamilton, Scotland.

Davie's father was a steelworker, and the young Davie was an ardent Rangers supporter whilst he attended Beckford Street Primary School and then Udston Primary School before finishing his education at St John's Grammar School. As an inside forward, Davie played football throughout his school years.

At local youth team Hamilton Avondale, he played in both the under 16 and under 18 teams and was then selected to represent Scotland's amateur league side.

When he left school, however, his first job was as an apprentice printer. But his footballing talent had not gone unnoticed, and several clubs, Rangers included, expressed an interest in the young lad, but it was Clydebank who first obtained his services, in 1974.

Three years later, in 1977, Cooper had moved to Rangers at the age of 21, where the winger would stay for 12 years and also be capped 22 times for the Scottish National team.

After Rangers, Cooper left to join Motherwell, a move that Rangers manager Graeme Souness lived to regret.

Davie Cooper is another player who is considered to be one of Scotland's finest footballers. His strength and elegant play together with superb ball control made him an invaluable member of the team creating opportunities, scoring goals and sending across pinpoint accurate passes. A natural left-footer, he would twist, turn, dip his shoulder and slip past opposition players without recourse to his right boot.

In 1975, Cooper, whose reserved nature led to his nickname "The Moody Blue", met Christine McMeekin and they married in 1980, Christine later giving birth to their daughter Nicola. The couple eventually separated.

Having retired from football in 1995, he began to coach young players, but on the morning of the 22nd of March 1995 he suffered a brain haemorrhage and died in the early hours of the 23rd of March. He was 39 years old. A statue was erected in his honour in 1999 at the Hamilton Palace Sports and Recreation Grounds.

Davie Cooper was inducted into the Scottish Football Hall of Fame.

RICHARD GOUGH

Charles Richard Gough was born on the 5th of April 1962 in Stockholm, Sweden. Richard's father was Scottish and young Richard grew up in South Africa, where he attended school at King Edward VII and Highlands North High School in Johannesburg.

Gough had already made his name as one of the most talented defenders before his career in Britain began in 1978, when he signed for Charlton Athletic before joining Dundee United in 1980.

The defender's Rangers adventure began in 1987, by which time he was already a Scotland national team player, eventually appearing for the squad 61 times until 1993, and becoming captain for Spurs. And endearing himself forever to Scottish fans when he scored the only goal in the 1-0 defeat of England in 1985.

Gough was a born leader, whose intelligence, intense focus and skilled reading of a game led him to become captain,

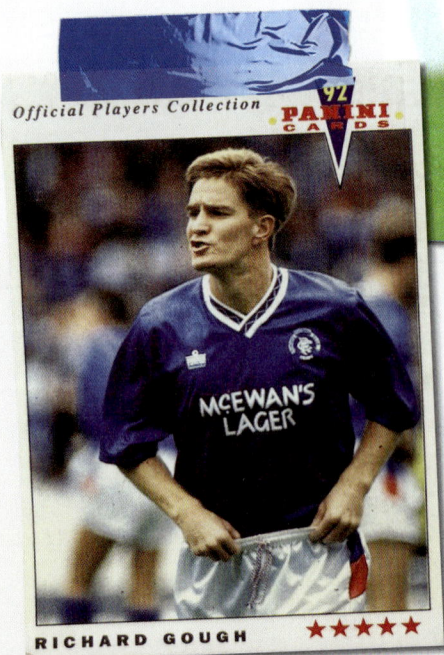

considered to be one of the best in a Rangers jersey, a member of the team that thrilled fans on their way to the Nine in a Row in the 1990s. He was coolheaded, fearless and always rose to the occasion, ready to put away the big goals in crucial moments in crucial matches.

Gough finally left Rangers in 1997 after 294 appearances.

Following a short period managing Livingston football club he became a Rangers ambassador.

SANDY JARDINE

William Sandy Pullar Jardine was born on the 31st of December 1948 in Edinburgh, Scotland.

Jardine, given the nickname 'Sandy' thanks to his hair colour, came in for early praise for his football skills at both Balgreen Primary School and Tynecastle Secondary School.

His professional career began in 1964 when the midfielder signed for Rangers, and he left the reserves in 1967 to join the first team at right-half.

Thanks to his speed, he could be relied on almost one hundred percent of the time to be in position when he was needed, and he took a pivotal role in the defence, where his strength and ability was inestimable, going on to make 674 appearances for the club. Such was his ability that he received SWFA Footballer of the Year award twice and was known as a man who gave everything for the club he loved.

Jardine finally left Rangers in 1982, by which time he had made 38 appearances for the Scottish national team. When he retired from football he returned to Rangers working in the public relations department and then as marketing and sales manager. He also stayed at the club during that difficult period of administration, organising the fighting fund.

Sandy and his wife Shona were parents to two children, Steven and Nicola.

His pride in Rangers and the part he played in their achievements are well known. Sadly, Sandy Jardine died on the 24th of April 2014 after losing his battle against cancer.

SANDY JARDINE AWARDS:

- SFWA Footballer of the Year, 1974-75, 1985-86
- Scottish Football Hall of Fame 2006
- Rangers FC Hall of Fame.

AND SOME OF THE EARLY HEROES

1936 SCOTTISH CUP AND GLASGOW CUP DOUBLE WINNING RANGERS TEAM

D. D. MEIKLEJOHN, Glasgow Rangers

DAVID MEIKLEJOHN

David Ditchburn Meiklejohn was born on the 12th of December 1900 in Govan, Scotland. He joined Rangers in 1919 and spent his entire career with the club until he retired in 1936 after 494 appearances. Playing at centre-back/right-half, Meiklejohn also played for the Scottish National team making 15 appearances and being named captain six times between 1922 and 1933. With Rangers, he won 13 Scottish League Championships, five Scottish Cups and eight Glasgow Cups.

Meiklejohn lived in a two-bedroom apartment just 100 yards from Ibrox and is considered to be the best captain of the pre-WW2 generation and one of the finest half-backs in Scotland, a tactical genius, and in contention as one of the best Rangers players ever.

When an ankle injury forced his retirement, he worked as a reporter for the Daily Record newspaper and became manager of Partick Thistle in 1947.

At the age of 58 Meiklejohn - who will always remain in the memory of the Rangers faithful because of the heroic penalty he scored against Celtic under intense emotional pressure in the Scottish Cup final at Hampden Park on the 14th of April 1928 - collapsed and died of a heart attack on the way to hospital on the 22nd of August 1959.

David Meiklejohn was inducted into the Rangers Hall of Fame in 2009.

THE PLAYERS

A POLICEMAN HELPING THE GLASGOW RANGERS STALWART AND SCOTLAND CAPTAIN, GEORGE YOUNG, FROM THE PITCH AFTER SCOTLAND BEAT ENGLAND 3-1 AT WEMBLEY

GEORGE YOUNG

George Lewis Young was born on the 27th of October 1922 in Grangemouth, Scotland.

Known as Corky because of the 'lucky' champagne cork that he always brought with him after his first International in 1943 against England, George Young's football trajectory began with Kirkintilloch Rob Roy Junior side. He began his Rangers' career in 1941 and captained Rangers to six Scottish League Championships, four Scottish Cup wins and two League Cup victories. He also became the first player to be capped 50 times for the Scottish National team. A true giant of a man at 6ft 2in in height, a defender who was a hard nut to crack but fair, Young played for Scotland on 54 occasions, chosen as captain for 48 of those matches.

Renowned for his unmatched ability to read a game and get into strong positions, also for his strength in airborne battles, he could send an accurate pass over long distances to set his teammates away on the attack. And he was the man who could withstand the pressure of the penalty kick at a crucial stage in game.

George Young left Rangers in 1957 after more than 700 appearances (booked just once for sensing an injustice against a teammate) and began a career as a hotelier. After a period of illness that left him in a wheelchair, Corky's death came on the 10th of January 1997 at the age of 74.

GEORGE YOUNG AWARDS:

- Scottish FA International Roll of Honour.

AND ONE OF THE

JAMES TAVERNIER

James Henry Tavernier was born on the 31st of October 1991 in Bradford, West Yorkshire, England. He was only nine years old when he joined the Leeds United youth system spending six seasons with the club, mostly in a central midfield position.

In 2008 he began playing for Newcastle United and after several years on loan to a variety of English clubs, he joined Rangers in 2015. He has now played 238 games for the club scoring 57 goals.

He became captain of the team in July 2018, and his opening goal in the Europa League semi-final against RB Leipzig in May 2022, earned him a place in the hearts of all Rangers fans.

Tavernier sets himself high standards, and his resilience, solid defensive performances and sometimes brilliant displays, which have been called "swashbuckling", have resulted in 57 goals.

THE PLAYERS

JAMES TAVERNIER AWARDS:

- PFA Scotland Players Player of the Year, 2020–2021
- PFA Scotland Team of the Year, 2015–16 Scottish Championship
- Scottish Championship Player of the Month, August 2015
- Scottish Premier Player of the Month, September 2020, November 2020
- Scottish Professional Football League Goal of the Season, 2015–16
- UEFA Europa league top scorer, 2021–22
- UEFA Europa league squad of the season, 2021–22

TOP PLAYERS OF 2022

THE MANAGERS

As is the case with the players, there are many managers who guided Rangers and deserve mention, too many to detail here, however, among them those who served well, if briefly, Steven Gerrard or the inimitable Ally McCoist for example. There were the early greats, too, the two Williams, Wilton and Waddell. Here are just a handful of the others.

BILL STRUTH

William Struth was born on the 16th of June 1875 in Leith, Scotland. His father was a stonemason and he and his wife Isabella Cunningham named their first born William after his father. Although William Junior originally worked as a stonemason, too, and an athlete until in 1908, he became the trainer at Clyde football club moving to Rangers in 1914 as assistant manager.

In 1920 he took over as manager at the club, and he immediately applied his disciplinarian values to the players as well. Yet he also employed skilled psychological insights and knew how each player needed to be treated. But if players failed to respond in the way he required, he was ruthless in casting them aside.

He went on to become one of the most successful football managers in the history of the British Isles, claiming an astonishing 30 major trophies. He claimed 18 Scottish League Championships, a record, 10 Scottish Cups and 2 Scottish League Cups. He also won nineteen Glasgow Cups and seventeen Glasgow Merchant Charity Cups.

Bill married Catherine Forbes, who died in 1941. Contracting gangrene, part of his leg was amputated in 1952. He lived to the age of 81 and died on the 21st of September 1956.

Bill Struth will also be remembered for the immortal lines that have become a credo at Rangers FC: "To be a Ranger is to sense the sacred trust of upholding all that such a name means in this shrine of football. They must be true in their conception of what the Ibrox tradition seeks from them. No true Ranger has ever failed in the tradition set him."

JOCK WALLACE

John Martin Bokas Wallace was born on the 6th of September 1935 in Wallyford, Scotland.

Jock Wallace began his professional career in 1952 with Workington and went on to play as goalkeeper in a series of English and Scottish clubs. Wallace carved himself a unique niche in British football by being the only player ever to play in the Scottish, English and Welsh Cups in the same season, 1966-67. With Hereford United, he played in the Welsh Cup and the FA Cup and then, moving to Berwick Rangers, he played in the Scottish Cup.

Retiring from football in 1969, Jock then managed Berwick Rangers for three years before moving onto Rangers FC in 1972, where he would stay until 1978. He would manage the team for a second spell from 1983 until 1986, although without being able to recreate the same sparkling success that had characterised his first management period.

Wallace was responsible for bringing the silverware back to Rangers during the mid-1970s, ending Celtic's domination of the period and their nine-in-a-row League run, and gaining Rangers' first title for 11 years. Rightly called "a giant of a man", Wallace's reign continued until he abruptly left the club for a reason that was unknown at the time to the general public and remains unknown to this day.

Renowned for his fiery temper, he would pour hellfire over players who displeased him and scare the living daylights out of them, yet despite his ruthless training methods, the majority of those who played under him would not have wanted to find themselves anywhere else but within sight of that clenched Wallace fist.

Jock Wallace died on the 24th of July 1996 after a battle with Parkinson's disease.

WALLACE WARNING FOR 'BLUE' RANGERS

GRAEME SOUNESS

Graeme James Souness was born on the 6th of May 1953 in Edinburgh, Scotland.

Graham's career as a professional began at Tottenham Hotspur in 1968 at the age of 15, and he was then sold to Middlesbrough in 1972. By then, his commitment to the game and sophisticated skills began to draw the attention of other clubs, and his ascent to greatness began in 1978 when the 5ft 11in midfielder joined Liverpool.

After two years at Sampdoria, he came to Rangers in 1986, and there he would stay until 1991, retiring from the club and from the game as a player after 50 goals. Souness also played for the Scottish National team 54 times between 1974 and 1986.

It was in 1986 that Souness became Rangers' first ever player-manager, arriving at the club at a time when there had not been a league title victory since 1978. Souness began to look to England to bolster the ranks of the Rangers team and so initiated what came to be known as the "Souness Revolution". The revitalised Rangers squad was soon back challenging for the top spots in every competition, and under his guidance, the club brought in three Scottish League titles and four Scottish League Cups. Only the chance to manage Liverpool Football Club tempted him away from Scotland once more. It was while at Liverpool that chest pains warned him that all was not well with his health. Doctors diagnosed coronary heart disease and he was subjected to open-heart surgery. He suffered a heart attack in 2015 and has since become an ambassador for the British Heart Foundation.

His tenure at Rangers was an outstanding success, even though he had courted controversy not only with his fiercely provocative nature on the sidelines and elsewhere, which he later described as almost "out of order", but by hiring Mo Johnston, perhaps the most high-profile Catholic player who had ever played at Rangers up until that time and who had also played for Celtic. "I had absolutely no fear and that just shows you how naive I was. I didn't know what I was getting into", Souness commented later.

Once his management of Newcastle United ended in 2006, Graeme Souness took up football commentary on television.

Souness married Danielle Wilson in 1984. Danielle already had a young daughter and she and Graeme had three more children together before they divorced after separation in 1989.

In 1994 he married Karen Souness. Karen brought two children of her own into the relationship and gave birth to a son with Graeme.

AMONG GRAEME SOUNESS'S AWARDS ARE:

- Premier League Manager of the Month, October 1996, April 1997
- European Cup Golden Boot, 1980-81
- Scotland national football team roll of honour, 1985
- Football League 100 Legends
- Liverpool 100 players who shook the Kop
- English Football Hall of Fame
- Scottish Football Hall of Fame
- Rangers Hall of Fame

WALTER SMITH

Walter Ferguson Smith, OBE, was born on the 24th of February 1948 in Lanark, Scotland. His early life took place in Glasgow, and when he left school he joined the South of Scotland Electricity Board. It was with the junior league team in Ashfield that Walter Smith began his football career in the 1960s.

His management career took off when he was appointed to take over the Scotland under 18 team in 1978, and he came to Rangers in 1986 as assistant manager to Graeme Souness. It was in 1991 that his chance came to take over at the helm when Graeme Souness left for Liverpool, and he guided the team for his first period in charge, which would last until 1998.

Smith would go on to help the team to 6 successive league titles throwing in a domestic treble in 1992-93 for good measure. By the time he left Rangers, the club had won the Scottish Cup and the League Cup three times. In the 1996-97 season, the Gers also matched Celtic's nine successive League Championships. The reverse of the coin was the £50m spent in transfer fees, which exceeded the payments made by any other British club. And over this period, the club was slowly sinking into a quagmire of debt that would eventually choke it.

Poor results in the European competitions led to Smith feeling the weight of disappointment at Ibrox, and he left the club at the end of the 1997-98 season.

Almost 10 years on, he was back, taking charge of his first match on the 13th of January 2007 and enjoying the 5-0 victory against Dundee United. He would stay at the helm until the end of the 2010-11 season after which the club went into administration.

By then, the Light Blues had won three successive Premier League titles, and two more Scottish Cups. In the 2007-08 season, they had won a Domestic Double and gone through to the final of the UEFA Cup under his stewardship.

Walter Smith and his wife Ethel had two sons together, Neil and Steven. Early in 2021, he went into hospital and on the 26th of October that year he succumbed to cancer at the age of 73.

Smith was remembered as "... a formidable manager and a formidable man", who possessed strength and presence, which were contributory factors in his enormously successful professional career.

WALTER SMITH AWARDS.

- Scottish Premier League Manager of the Year, 2007-08, 2009-10
- SFWA Manager of the Year, 1991-92, 1992-93, 1993-94, 1995-96, 1996-97, 2007-08, 2009-10
- FPA Scotland Manager of the Year, 2009-10
- Premier League Manager of the Month, September 1999
- Scottish Premier League Manager of the Month, August 2007, January 2008, March 2008, April 2009, December 2009, August 2010
- Glasgow Caledonian University, Andre Gregory, 2012 (Honorary Doctorate in Recognition of His Achievements in Scottish Football)
- Officer of the Order of the British Empire, 1997

WILLIAM WILTON

By 1889, he had become the match secretary for the first team and later the treasurer as well. Ten years passed before the moment arrived for him to stamp his name indelibly into the Rangers history books when in 1899, the year the club acquired limited company status, he was selected to become the first manager of Rangers FC in addition to the role of club secretary. He would remain at the helm until his death in 1920. He also oversaw the move to Ibrox that same year of 1899.

The team lost just one game that first season, and during his occupation of the hot seat he guided the club to 7 Scottish League titles, a Scottish Cup victory, in 1902-03, and 9 Glasgow Cups. Wilton had set the points for the club's future successful direction.

William Wilton died in 1920 after the season ended when the yacht he was sailing in ran into difficulties and Wilton drowned before the boat could be moored. He was just 54 years of age.

William Wilton was born on the 9th of June 1865 in Largs, Ayrshire, Scotland. His mother, Janet, was a weaver and his father, James, was a stonemason. William's first waged employment was as a mercantile clerk in the sugar industry.

William joined Rangers in 1883, the year he married his wife, Catherine, but never quite made the grade as a first-team player. Instead, he found his niche as a talented organiser and administrator as the secretary for the youth and reserve squads.

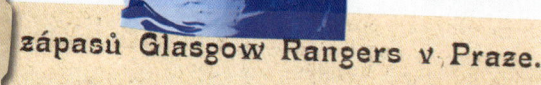

Mužstvo Glasgow Rangers.

1904

THE MANAGERS

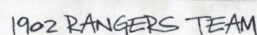

1902 RANGERS TEAM

CARTOON FROM 1904 COMMENTING UPON THE OLD FIRM'S DOMINATION OF SCOTTISH FOOTBALL

1902 IBROX DISASTER

THE STATISTICS

POSITION IN THE LEAGUE:

SCOTTISH FOOTBALL LEAGUE (SFL)

1890-91 - 1
1891/92 - 5
1892/93 - 2

DIVISION ONE

1893/94 - 4
1894/95 - 3
1895/96 - 2
1896/97 - 3
1897/98 - 2
1898/99 - 1
1899/1900 - 1
1900/01 - 1
1901/02 - 1
1902/03 - 3
1903/04 - 3
1904/05 - 2
1905/06 - 4
1906/07 - 3
1907/08 - 3
1908/09 - 4
1909/10 - 3
1910/11 - 1
1911/12 - 1
1912/13 - 1
1913/14 - 2

WORLD WAR I

1919/20 - 1
1920/21 - 1
1921/22 - 2
1922/23 - 1
1923/24 - 1
1924/25 - 1
1925/26 - 6
1926/27 - 1
1927/28 - 1
1928/29 - 1
1929/30 - 1
1930/31 - 1
1931/32 - 2
1932/33 - 1
1933/34 - 1
1934/35 - 1
1935/36 - 2
1936/37 - 1
1937/38 - 3
1938/39 - 1

WORLD WAR II

SFL DIVISION A.

1946/47 - 1
1947/48 - 2
1948/49 - 1
1949/50 - 1
1950/51 - 2
1951/52 - 2
1952/53 - 1
1953/54 - 4
1954/55 - 3

SFL DIVISION ONE.

1955/56 - 1
1956/57 - 1
1957/58 - 2
1958/59 - 1
1959/60 - 3
1960/61 - 1
1961/62 - 2

THE STATISTICS

1962/63 – 1
1963/64 – 1
1964/65 – 5
1965/66 – 2
1966/67 – 2
1967/68 – 2
1968/69 – 2
1969/70 – 2
1970/71 – 4
1971/72 – 3
1972/73 – 2
1973/74 – 3
1974/75 – 1

SCOTTISH PREMIER DIVISION

1975/76 – 1
1976/77 – 2
1977/78 – 1
1978/79 – 2
1979/80 – 5
1980/81 – 3
1981/82 – 3
1982/83 – 4
1983/84 – 4
1984/85 – 4
1985/86 – 5
1986/87 – 1
1987/88 – 3
1988/89 – 1
1989/90 – 1

PREMIER DIVISION

1990/91 – 1
1991/92 – 1
1992/93 – 1
1993/94 – 1
1994/95 – 1
1995/96 – 1
1996/97 – 1
1997/98 – 2

SCOTTISH PREMIER LEAGUE

1998/99 – 1
1999/2000 – 1
2000/01 – 2
2001/02 – 2
2002/03 – 1
2003/04 – 2
2004/05 – 1
2005/06 – 3
2006/07 – 2
2007/08 – 2
2008/09 – 1
2009/10 – 1
2010/11 – 1
2011/12 – 2

THIRD DIVISION

2012/13 – 1

LEAGUE ONE

2013/14 – 1

CHAMPIONSHIP

2014/15 – 3
2015/16 – 1

PREMIERSHIP

2016/17 – 3
2017/18 – 3
2018/19 – 2
2019/20 – 2
2020/21 – 1
2021/22 – 2

MORE STATS

CUP COMPETITIONS:

SCOTTISH CUP WINNERS: (34):

1894, 1897, 1898, 1903, 1928, 1930, 1932, 1934, 1935, 1936, 1948, 1949, 1950, 1953, 1960, 1962, 1963, 1964, 1966, 1973, 1976, 1978, 1979, 1981, 1992, 1993, 1996, 1999, 2000, 2002, 2003, 2008, 2009, 2022

SCOTTISH LEAGUE CUP WINNERS: (27)

1947, 1949, 1961, 1962, 1964, 1965, 1971, 1976, 1978, 1979, 1982, 1984, 1985, 1987, 1988, 1988-89, 1990-91, 1992-93, 1993-94, 1996-97, 1998-99, 2001-02, 2002-03, 2004-05, 2007-08, 2009-10, 2010-11

UEFA CUP WINNERS:

1972

SCOTTISH CHALLENGE CUP WINNERS:

2015-16

GLASGOW CUP WINNERS: (44):

1893, 1894, 1897, 1898, 1900, 1901, 1902, 1911, 1912, 1913, 1914, 1918, 1919, 1922, 1923, 1924, 1925, 1930, 1932, 1933, 1934, 1936, 1937, 1938, 1940, 1942, 1943, 1944, 1945, 1948, 1950, 1954, 1957, 1958, 1960, 1969, 1971, 1975, 1976, 1979, 1983, 1985, 1986, 1987

GLASGOW MERCHANTS CHARITY CUP WINNERS: (32):

1878-79, 1896-97, 1899-1900, 1903-04, 1905-06, 1906-07, 1908-09, 1910-11, 1918-19, 1921-22, 1922-23, 1924-25, 1927-28, 1928-29, 1929-30, 1930-31, 1931-32, 1932-33, 1933-34, 1938-39, 1939-40, 1940-41, 1941-42, 1943-44, 1944-45, 1945-46, 1946-47, 1947-48, 1950-51, 1954-55, 1956-57, 1959-60

THE STATISTICS

The Glasgow Rangers players celebrate victory after the Scottish Cup final match against arch-rivals Glasgow Celtic played at the new Hampden Park in Glasgow, Scotland. The match finished in a 0-1 win for Glasgow Rangers and they achieved the domestic treble, 29 May 1999